# Sing!

## Learn How To
## Sing Like An Idol:
Vocal Techniques
For Modern Singers

**Mark W. Curran**
with a Foreword by
David Foster

NMD Books
Simi Valley, CA

Visit our Web site at http://www.NMDbooks.com.

Sing! Learn How To Sing Like An Idol:
Vocal Techniques For Modern Singers

ISBN: 978-1-936828-17-3  (Softcover)


First Edition March 2011

# Table Of Contents

# Introduction

What could be more fun and more expressive than singing?

Since the beginning of his ascent, man has been a singing creature expressing the full range of his emotion and intellect through song and voice. Much like drama and literature, singing has been with us for centuries and today holds the distinction of being one of the most dominant expressions of artistic ability.

The successes of television programs such as "American Idol" and "America's Got Talent" are just one indication of the popularity and interest in singing idols.

Our pop culture seems to revolve around the latest singing stars. With every printed, televised and digitally tweeted update our society hangs in apt fascination of not only the singer's latest hits, but their most recent loves, decadences, arrests and occasionally, their accomplishments.

No matter how lofty or modest your goals in singing are, one must start with the basics.

As a professional vocalist, I have always felt the need for a comprehensive coursebook in the art of singing. Although there are a great many books on the subject of singing, (some good, some bad) each one that I pursued in my own personal quest for vocal excellence seemed to be missing something.

One book would examine the mechanics of singing, while another would address only the exercises and give no consideration of where the singer could go once the techniques were mastered.

Almost all of them seemed to become overly complex when simplification would have sufficed.

Many books seemed lacking in just how and where to apply the principles learned, and further, completely ignored the elements of marketing needed to approach or even understand the marketplace.

I felt there needed to be a book that addressed the concerns of today's modern singer in a more holistic way, both novice and professional.

The music business has gone through tumultuous change in recent years, one which affects the opportunities for professional singers. The marketplace is evolving, older markets are maturing, and new ones are emerging.

While these changes may not affect the mechanics of singing, they do impact what direction the singer may take in applying what has been learned.

This brings us to the subject of marketing.

While marketing one's self as a singer is a subject that does require a book of its own to completely explore in depth, this volume will touch on some of the more important aspects needed for the vocalist to get a healthy overview and a head start on pursuing a career in professional singing.

The main thing to remember is to have fun and enjoy singing.

In my view, nothing else will bring you greater joy, or take you as far as you want to go.


Mark W. Curran
Los Angeles
2011

# Foreword by David Foster

During my years as a professional arranger, vocalist and musician I've met a great many singers in various stages of their development. While many had classical training and backgrounds in the art of proper singing, some did not.

It become apparent to me even in the early part of my own career that even those who had proper training in singing had developed bad habits that were difficult to break, and which resulted in fatigued voices, laryngitis, and worse.

To those who came to me without any experience or training, I was faced to start from scratch. This seemed an almost easier task in that their minds were fresh and open to new ideas, but nonetheless it was a hard road made even more difficult by a lack of decent books on the subject.

So it came as a delight and surprise to me when Mark W. Curran came to me and asked me to write this forward. On reading his book, I came to realize that this was the missing link.

In my view, this work represents a breakthrough in books on vocal study, one which addresses the whole singer, not just the mechanics of singing.

There are a great many other considerations than just singing that impact today's modern singer, and I believe this book addresses these concerns admirably.

The other thing I might mention is that in today's society and in the music business in general, youth is revered. Although there is a great deal of hoopla made of the young vocalists, it is never too late to start singing, whether you are in your teens or are in your eighties.

As Mark has indicated here, it's the journey, not the destination that is important.

The enjoyment comes in the doing.

No matter what your age, background or denomination, go after your dreams and remember that anything is possible.

This book will help you in that pursuit.


David Foster
Hollywood
2011

# What Makes An Idol?

In today's celebrity-infatuated world, it seems the question were never more intriguing. What exactly makes an idol? What qualities seem to come together at the right zenith to propel a singer to the heights of worldwide stardom? What keeps them there?

We can only guess, for if we knew the definitive answer to this, we could capture lightning in a bottle. Since our subject here pertains to singers, one thing we can say for sure.

To become an idol, or at least sing like one, you have to master the art of singing.

This means learning the rudiments of your instrument, and then learning how to use it in a way that incites and impassions audiences.

Once there, you must maintain your humanity, keep your ego in check, and reach for the stars.

This book is your first step toward achieving that goal.

## Do I Need To Take Vocal Lessons From A Teacher?

Learning the proper technique of singing without a live teacher can be a trial and error experience, and it's quite easy to develop bad habits along the way.

I always advise singers that if they can afford the expense and time of live teaching lessons, to do so if for no other reason than to be sure the techniques they are using are being executed properly.

The voice is a sensitive instrument, and must always be treated as such. A good vocal instructor can go a long way toward showing you what the proper technique for singing is, and how to get the most out of your voice, as well as the proper care and rest of the vocal cords.

That being said, it is not absolutely essential to take live lessons from a teacher. There are a great many books out there on learning the proper way, and some even include audio cd's to practice along with for vocal exercises.

But, to be safe, at least a few introductory "live" lessons might serve you well in making sure you are off on the right foot.

However, I would advise you to read my treatise in the final chapter of this book titled "Beware Charlatans," for the vocal instruction world both online and offline is rife with predators laying in wait to empty your pockets and leave you for dead.

Now, let us begin!

# I. THE BASICS

## How the Voice Works

The production of voice involves a complex set of tasks requiring the coordination of many muscles and sensory nerves. Simply producing a simple syllable such as \a\ involves the use of rib and stomach muscles in coordination with the diaphragm to control airflow combined with muscles in the neck, voice box, upper throat, and mouth to modulate that air into sound.

Sensory feedback from nerves in the throat and voice box, as well as sensory cues from the nerves of hearing also are involved in the processing of that sound to form the proper syllable. All of this complex coordination is performed instantly, subconsciously, and continuously during speech.

As the system is complex, there are many things that can go wrong with it. Anything from scarring of the vocal cords to lung problems can produce hoarseness. Below is a conceptual framework for how the human voice is created.

The human voice can be looked at as if it were a set of tunes played from a complex musical instrument. The basic setup for the production of voice involves three components. The first is the power generator.

This consists of the lungs, which produce a column of air with a certain force. The force or pressure produced depends on the capacity of the lungs to store air prior to exhalation, and the strength of the muscles used to exhale that air. Problems with lung capacity or muscle strength can weaken the power generator, and may lead to certain kinds of hoarseness.

The second component in voice production is a vibrating structure. This consists of the vocal cords. To produce voice, the vocal cords are brought together. As the column of air generated in the lungs rushes through the windpipe, the vocal cords vibrate to produce a tone. Different tones can be produced by varying the tension on the vocal

12

cords. Interference with proper motion or vibration of the vocal cords causes certain forms of hoarseness.

Once a tone is created, it needs to be modified to produce a proper voice. This involves the third component, the resonance chamber. Te resonance chamber consists of the upper part of the throat, the nose, and the mouth. Modifications of the configuration of these areas alter the voice to produce speech.

# How The Body Produces Sound

The human voice consists of sound made by a human being using the vocal folds for talking, singing, laughing, crying, screaming, etc. Its frequency ranges from 200 to 7000 Hz. The human voice is specifically that part of human sound production in which the vocal folds (vocal cords) are the primary sound source.

Generally speaking, the mechanism for generating the human voice can be subdivided into three parts; the lungs, the vocal folds within the larynx, and the articulators. The lung (the pump) must produce adequate airflow and air pressure to vibrate vocal folds (this air pressure is the fuel of the voice).

The vocal folds (vocal cords) are a vibrating valve that chops up the airflow from the lungs into audible pulses that form the laryngeal sound source. The muscles of the larynx adjust the length and tension of the vocal folds to 'fine tune' pitch and tone. The articulators (the parts of the vocal tract above the larynx consisting of tongue, palate, cheek, lips, etc.) articulate and filter the sound emanating from the larynx and to some degree can interact with the laryngeal airflow to strengthen it or weaken it as a sound source.

The vocal folds, in combination with the articulators, are capable of producing highly intricate arrays of sound. The tone of voice may be modulated to suggest emotions such as anger, surprise, or happiness.

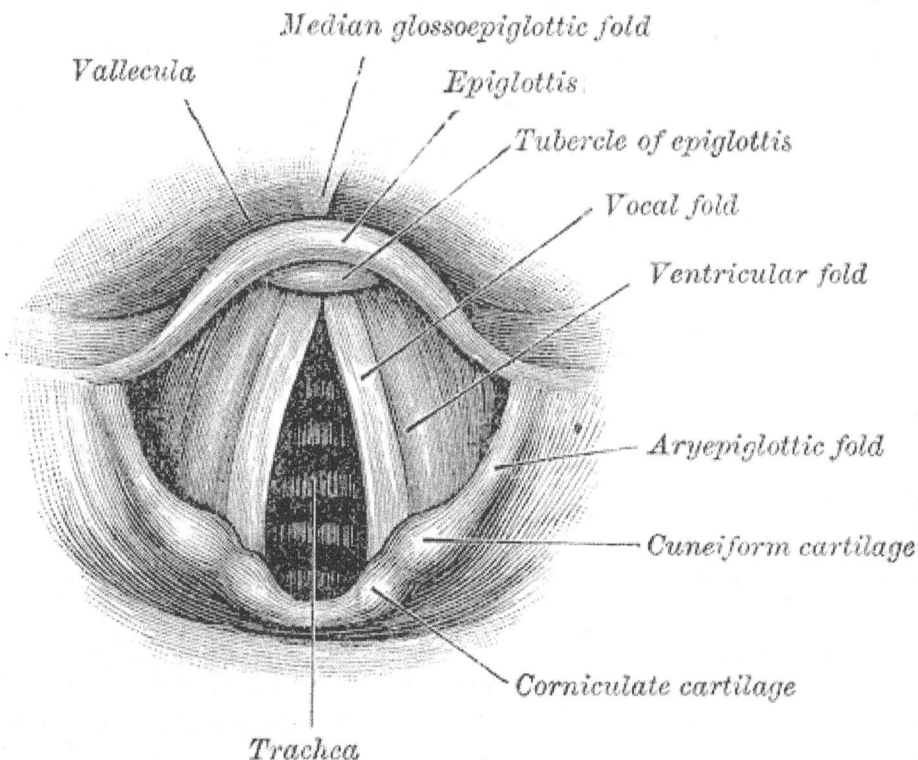

*A labeled anatomical diagram of the vocal folds or cords.*

# Breathing Basics For Singing

Normal breathing involves a shallow inhalation and an even exhalation followed by a pause before it all starts again. But when you sing, breath control means taking your breathing off autopilot. You not only need to inhale quickly and exhale slowly as you sing the phrases of a song, but you also need to maintain proper posture.

Breathing in this manner provides you with the breath control that you need to sing efficiently. However, because controlled breathing doesn't come naturally to you, you need to train your body to breathe for singing. Keep reading to walk through the breathing basics.

# Discovering Your Singing Breath

The easiest way to find out how you should breathe for singing is simply by feeling it. Being able to visualize and feel the proper way to breathe helps make the process more natural for you, too.

Inhalation refers to air moving into your body — breathing in. Exhalation is when you exhale or blow out the air. You exhale when you speak or sing.

## Inhaling to Sing

Singing songs requires getting a full breath quickly — a quick inhalation — because the orchestra can't wait five minutes for you to find the air. So knowing how your body feels when you inhale helps you to get air in your body quickly to sing the next phrase. Use the following exercise to explore your own inhalation. Get a feel for how your body should move when you inhale and exhale.

1. Pretend that air is really heavy as you inhale. Visualize it weighing fifty pounds and let it fall low into your body.

2. Let it fall lower than your belly button. Explore this sensation.

3. Then let the breath fall in faster. Still visualize it being heavy but let it fall quickly into your body.

4. You can also fill your lungs as if you were going to blow up a balloon. You will feel your abdomen and lower back expand.

This sensation of quickly filling your lungs with air is how you properly inhale for singing.

Yawning happens all the time when working on breath control. The body gets confused with the different amount of air coming in, and you yawn. Voice students yawn plenty during lessons and are embarrassed at first. Don't worry — it's okay to yawn when you're working on your breathing.

# Exhaling to sing

Singing means that you have to control your exhalation. You want to have a sustained and smooth exhalation. This control helps you to sing those demanding high notes and long slow phrases.

To explore exhalation, blow a feather around the room. If you have a spotless house, you'll have to use an imaginary feather.

1. Try to blow the feather really high up in the air and use a long stream of breath to get it to go up.

2. Try not to collapse your chest as you blow the feather.

3. While chasing the feather with your breath, notice what moves in your body as you exhale. You should feel that your abdomen has slowly returned to normal and that your chest has stayed in the same position the whole time.

4. At the end of the exhalation, you should feel the need to immediately inhale again.

# Posture

The singing process functions best when certain physical conditions of the body exist. The ability to move air in and out of the body freely and to obtain the needed quantity of air can be seriously affected by the posture of the various parts of the breathing mechanism.

A sunken chest position will limit the capacity of the lungs, and a tense abdominal wall will inhibit the downward travel of the diaphragm. Good posture allows the breathing mechanism to fulfill its basic function efficiently without any undue expenditure of energy. Good posture also makes it easier to initiate phonation and to tune the resonators as proper alignment prevents unnecessary tension in the body.

Vocal pedagogists have also noted that when singers assume good posture it often provides them with a greater sense of self assurance and poise while performing. Audiences also tend to respond better to singers with good posture. Habitual good posture also ultimately improves the overall health of the body by enabling better blood circulation and preventing fatigue and stress on the body.

There are eight components of the ideal singing posture:

1. Feet slightly apart
2. Legs straight but knees unlocked
3. Hips facing straight forward
4. Spine aligned
5. Abdomen flat
6. Chest comfortably forward
7. Shoulders down and back
8. Head facing straight forward

# Breath Support

Natural breathing has three stages: a breathing-in period, a breathing out period, and a resting or recovery period; these stages are not usually consciously controlled. Within singing there are four stages of breathing: a breathing-in period (inhalation); a setting up controls period (suspension); a controlled exhalation period (phonation); and a recovery period.

These stages must be under conscious control by the singer until they become conditioned reflexes. Many singers abandon conscious controls before their reflexes are fully conditioned which ultimately leads to chronic vocal problems.

# Vibrato

Vibrato is used by singers (and many instrumentalists; for instance, string instruments that are played with a bow can produce vibrato tones) in which a sustained note wavers very quickly and consistently between a higher and a lower pitch, giving the note a slight quaver. Vibrato is the pulse or wave in a sustained tone. Vibrato occurs naturally, and is the result of proper breath support and a relaxed vocal apparatus.[citation needed] Some singers use vibrato as a means of expression. Many successful artists have built a career on deep, rich vibrato.

# Resonance

Elements of Vocal Chords in Singing Resonance

The vocal chords in singing resonance have three elements in common to all musical instruments. A motor, a vibrator and a resonator. Additionally the human vocal chords have one more element which no instrument has and that is an Articulator.

Motor: Lungs and the respiratory muscles.
Vibrator: Vocal chords.
Resonator: Throat, mouth, nasal and head cavities.
Articulator: Tongue, lips, teeth and palate.

These elements are unique to each individual and, its size and capacity to perform also varies from person to person. But without doubt each individual's capacity has a unique beauty of its own. Since each person has a unique set of elements, it falls on him to develop its capabilities to the fullest extent and make use of its potential. With the strengthening, developing and modulating of these variables a human being can express feelings such as pleasure, pain, anger, grief, doubt , courage, fear etc with his voice and tonal  quality. No instrument on earth can produce such a variety of emotions.

The quality and power of resonance can be explained with the example of a tuning fork. When you vibrate a tuning fork, you can see the vibration but you cannot hear anything if it is held in air. But if you rest it on a table, or a plate, glass or on the bridge of a violin then the tones of the tuning fork will be distinctly heard to a long distance.

Similarly the vocal chords by itself cannot be heard without the aid of the other elements. When the vocal chords vibrate and combines with vibration of the air in the nasal and head cavities which forms the resonance chambers, the sound is formed and heard to the distance it is thrown and in the tonal quality and color it is formed depending on each individual.

Tone is the result of rapid periodic vibration. The pitch of tone depends upon number of vibrations in a given period; loudness of tone depends upon amplitude of the vibrations; quality of tone depends upon form of vibrations; and form of vibrations depends upon the resonator.

# Pitch

## What is Pitch?

Your singing pitch is the frequency of sound, e.g. high or low. Singing pitch is an objective measurement, and a specific pitch will sound the same whether a voice or instrument produces it. Notes represent the pitches most commonly used in music.

It is very difficult—and rare—to have perfect pitch. Some are born with a natural sense of pitch, while others must train their ears to memorize a note (such as middle C) and base other pitches off from that note. The latter technique is the best way to improve your ability to recognize pitch, and can be practiced and perfected over time.

Ear Training or Pitch Exercises are the terms used to describe the method of teaching and learning how to identify a note and sing in tune with the note or chord that is played.

Q. Why do I need to learn how to pitch a note to the music?
If you want to learn to sing or play an instrument it is essential to be able to sing the correct notes in the right place (and at the right time!). Ideally a singer should be able to recognize the key being played and sing any one of the notes within the chord or scale without sounding sharp or flat (unless that is the effect you require for the song!!).

Q. My friend can do this and she hasn't had lessons - but I can't - why is this?

Some people are born with an excellent 'ear' for music and are naturally talented, but most singers need to learn and practice the art before it becomes second nature.

Q. How can I tell if I am on pitch or not?

Record yourself singing along to a song that you know well and listen back to your efforts - are the notes you sing melodic, are they exactly the same as the singers or do they sound harsh, sharp or flat? If the latter is the case then you are not singing 'on pitch'. You can also try recording yourself singing our online scales. If you are singing in key then the notes you sing will sound like the notes that are played.

Q. What is 'Perfect Pitch?'

This is the term used to describe someone who can sing (or play) the notes (or chords) along with the music without reading the sheet music. It is also used to describe the ability to sing any note on request without hearing the note played by an instrument. Some people are born with this ability - others need to learn and practice to become competent.

Q. I Can't Pitch - Am I Tone Deaf?

Unlikely - very few people are really 'Tone Deaf' which is the term used to describe someone who appears to lack the ability to differentiate between one note (or chord) from another - This is extremely rare! Most people who think they are 'Tone Deaf' just need to learn how to listen and practice their pitching skills. It takes some people longer than others but it CAN be learned.

Q. How can I learn to pitch correctly?

The key to recognizing notes, chords and intervals is repeated listening and singing back.

## Consonants and Vowels

You've probably heard someone sing but couldn't understand very much. This is really bad when the song is in English or a language that you speak. By making your vowels and consonants specific, you can make yourself easily understood when singing.

Many voice teachers spend ages training their students to pronounce vowels and consonants in an exaggerated, hyper-enunciated way. The reason is that words often sound different when sung than when spoken. Singing depends on vowel sounds, with only a minor role played by consonants. Yet without the correct articulation provided by consonants, the words of song lyrics can be lost.

• Try this singing vowels exercise.

1. Stand in front of a mirror with your mouth open in a relaxed oval (not too wide).

2. Make the following vowel sounds without moving your lips or jaw.
ah ay eh ee i oh uh oo
Feel the way your throat and tongue move to create the different vowel sounds.

3. Now, allow yourself to move your mouth and say the vowels again.
ah ay eh ee i oh uh oo
See and hear the difference? The tone will most likely be less full and sound much less "professional."

When you are singing vowel sounds, then, you should always make sure that your mouth remains in the proper shape, and doesn't move. Don't drop or raise your jaw when you sing notes at either end of your range. You want your voice to sound natural ... and for you to feel natural while you're singing.

When you are singing a diphthong (a "compound vowel"), emphasize the initial vowel, adding only a hint of the second vowel sound at the end.

You do not want diphthongs forming where a single vowel sound should be. For example, if you sing the word "mine", you may find yourself singing "my-een", with an "ee" sound added after the "ah" sound.

In speech, when the escaping breath stream meets with an obstruction formed by the tongue, lips, teeth, or velum (soft palate), the resulting sound is called a consonant. The word comes from the Latin, con and sonare, meaning with sound" or "to sound together."

The dictionary defines it as "an articulate sound characterized by friction, squeezing, or stopping of the breath in some part of the mouth. It is usually sounded with a more open sound called a vowel:. In other words, a consonant is formed when the vowel chamber is blocked either partially or wholly.

As there are many vowel sounds possible through adjustments of the articulatory organs, so also can many consonants be formed by making the blockage in different ways.

Say slowly the following words, paying careful attention to the quality of consonants and the manner in which you produce them: to, do, pay, bee, key, go, lay, may, no, hang, red, vow, foe, see, rise, who, we, how, you, jug, chew, she, measure, thing, though. No doubt you noticed that, in order to pronounce some consonants, the column of air was at times completely stopped by the organs of speech and then released with a sudden explosion or puff; or sometimes it was only partially stopped, thus allowing the breath to escape gradually.

When the current of air is completely stopped and then released suddenly, sounds produced are called stop consonants or explosives.

They occur in the sounds t in to, d in do, p in pay, b in be, k in key, g in go, j in jug, and ch in chin. When the breath stream is only partly blocked, as in the sounds represented by r, 1, m, n, ng, th, f, v, s, z, y, sh, consonants called continuants are formed. Stop, or explosive consonants, are uttered quickly, but continuants may be lengthened or sounded continuously as the word implies.

In producing some consonants, the tip of the tongue obstructs the stream of breath; in others, the teeth and lips hinder the free emission of air, and sometimes the back of the tongue forms the blockage.

Consonants articulated by the two lips (as p, b, m) are called bi-labial sounds; those formed by the lower lip against the upper teeth (as f, v) are known as labio-dental sounds. Those produced by the tip or blade of the tongue against the teeth or teeth-ridge (as t, d, n, th) are classified as dental sounds.

Sounds articulated by the front of the tongue against the hard palate are termed palatal (as y), and those made by the back of the tongue against the soft palate (as k, g, and ng) are called velar sounds.

In most sounds, breath escapes through the oral cavity or mouth. However, in n, and ng air is released through the nose. For this reason, these sounds are often called nasal or resonant consonants.

## Breath Control

Good breathing technique is vital for voice control when singing. Singers will never be able to sing powerfully, sustain tone gracefully and sing emotionally without mastering proper breath control.

When you are taking a breath for singing, breathe from the bottom of your lungs up. When you develop good breathing habits for singing, you will be able to feel the breath all around your lower abdomen, not just the front. Your chest and shoulders may begin to lift as you take in your singing breath but do not let them lift or else the singing voice will sound strained and tensed. This article will explain the benefit of good breath control singing technique.

## Singing From the Diaphragm

You will be frustrated with your singing effort if shallow breathing is your breath control foundation. Shallow breathing is air stored on your upper lungs where your throat and the upper chest meet. Correct and good singing breathing technique begins with the diaphragm and also the breath support muscles. This is the reason why people are told to sing from the diaphragm.

The key to correct use of diaphragm and breath support muscles is the expansion of your lower abdomen when taking in your singing breath. You have to exercise and develop this technique until it comes naturally to you as a breathing habit even when you are breathing normally when not singing.

As you are practicing your singing breath control technique, do take notice of how much noise you make when you draw your breath. This is because many singers believe that a noisy breath is a deep breath which is not true.

When you breathe, take sips and not gulps. Silent breathing should be the aim of a good breathing habit. Again, practice silent breathing until it becomes your natural singing habit. Noisy breathing is usually caused by a throat that is constricted and it is an indication of shallow breathing contrary to what many singers think. If you are afraid to expand your abdomen when you are taking in your singing breath fearing the fat tummy look, this will lead to having tension in your abdomen and your diaphragm with its breath support muscles will not be working at its optimum peak.

Most singers are not even aware that they are holding all these tensions. One of the most important lessons to good singing technique is to relax so as to achieve the 'floating voice' quality. With so much tension in the singing support muscles, the relaxed floating voice will be difficult if not impossible to achieve. This tension is probably the result of years of stomach in chest out posture inculcated since young. At this point, let's perform a vocal exercise to correct bad breathing habits.

## Vocal Exercise

Start with taking a few quiet breaths. As you breathe in, expand your lower abdominals all around including the sides and the lower back. Make a mental note on how a quiet breath feels like.

Now release the air steadily and sing 'Ahhh' as you release the air with your stomach going back to its original position. Did you notice that the sound quality you produced is steadier and has a floating tone to it? It must be emphatically emphasized that the amount of air required for good singing is very little. Therefore, a proper amount of air attached to a note should be just adequate, nothing more, nothing less.

# Vocal Placement

One of the most difficult things to learn is vocal placement. "Don't" is the best advice here: don't sing excessively through the nose, don't muffle the voice by singing deep in the throat and don't forget to produce pure vowels while singing. Voice teachers often tell students to "sing through the mask" for the most desirable "bright" sound, but the sensation eludes many. It is simply an open sound that resonates through the mouth and palate.

# Vocal Power and Projection

To open up for bigger vocal sound, try to open up the area near the base of the tongue. This can be done by imagining the beginning of a yawn. This imaging opens up the singing pathway, keeps the tongue in the correct position and lifts the soft palate making your mouth shaped like a megaphone. A megaphone amplifies a small sound doesn't it? When your mouth is in this position, it will act like a megaphone.

With this megaphone like mouth structure, the back of the throat will naturally open up making the critical blend between the vocal tone colors of the upper and lower resonances possible. While you are singing, the inner structure of your mouth is constantly working, moving to fine tune the oral cavity until the feel and sound of any sustained note is just right.

The correct position of the mouth should thus be in a slight oval-like shape with the corners of the mouth drawn in and the jaw down. It is critical that your lips are relaxed. If your lips are tensed, tension will accumulate around the jaw and your mouth making your singing tone sounding tight and tensed which will make your listeners feeling uncomfortable, although they may not know why.

When your mouth is in this position, the jaw, tongue and the palate will more relaxed and will be responding to the direction of the inner ear. As you gain more experience, you will be sensitive to the feeling of the mouth cavity subtly adjusting to each vowel as it fits into the available space in your mouth.

All this amazing mechanism takes place just because of your imaging of the beginning of a yawn. However if you generate a full yawn, then the voice box will be lowered too much and that will create a new obstruction in your singing pathway rather than freeing up your voice so that you can have a big powerful singing voice.

Another source singing pathway blockage is your tongue. Just make sure that your tongue is relaxed and sits comfortably against the back of your bottom teeth. If your tongue pulls back, the airflow will be obstructed and will divide the mouth and throat into 2 resonators. On the other hand, it the tongue lift up too high, the mouth will be again be separated into two resonators, front and back.

Therefore the optimal mouth position when sustaining tone on a vowel for the big singing voice is a flat forward relaxed tongue position just behind the lower teeth oval mouth position and the imaging of the beginning of a yawn.

This is only one of the many singing techniques for getting a big powerful voice. It must be done in conjunction with other singing techniques such as correct use of the breath support system, proper use of your natural resonators and voice projection.

When the techniques are used to perfect combination, what follows naturally from here will be a bigger and a more powerful singing voice. To get that big powerful singing voice, regular vocal exercises to perfect the singing techniques is critical.

## Voice Projection

Voice projection is the act of using the voice strongly and clearly. It is actively employed as a technique to command attention and respect in a room. Teachers use this in a classroom to gain students' attention. Actors and singers use strong voice projection to be heard clearly places such as large theaters.

If you pay special attention to professional singers, you will begin to notice that all good singers possess voices that can boom and roar into the distance. Very few people are born with a natural booming voice that projects long distances; however, by practicing the proper voice

26

projection exercises, you can develop a strong and powerful voice that projects.

Special note: yelling is not the same as voice projecting. Yelling should never be used in singing. Yelling can cause serious physical damage to your vocal cords. When people yell, they are forcing air through the voice box. This is the number one cause of the development of vocal nodules, which is a serious physical ailment that needs surgical intervention to correct.

### Where Does Voice Projection Come From?
Whenever you sing a note, your vocal cords allow a certain amount of pressure to build up before the vocal cords are opened, releasing the pent up air to create a musical note. Louder notes are created with a stronger air pressure in the vocal cords. The vocal cords also open faster in order to release the air quicker.

Essentially, higher volume voice uses higher air pressure in conjunction with a quicker opening of the vocal cords. A lower volume voice uses a lower air pressure in conjunction with a slower opening of the vocal cords.

Strong voice projection is related to air pressure and your vocal cord opening rate. It is not related to how much air your exhale; this is why we specifically mention that you should not yell.

### How to Develop Stronger Voice Projection
In order to develop stronger voice projection, you must first strengthen the muscles inside the voice box. The voice box houses your vocal cords when you sing, and improved projective power and volume can be achieved by strengthening these muscles. A more muscular and robust voice box will allow you to create a higher air pressure, which produces louder notes.

# Voice Projection Exercise Materials:

### Swiss Ball (Workout Rubber Ball)

Strong voice projection is directly related to your posture. This exercise focuses on improving posture to strengthen your voice projection.

1. Kneel on the ground, facing the rubber Swiss ball
2. Lean forward until your stomach is on the ball. Place your feet on the ground behind you. Your hands    should be placed on the ground in front of you.
3. Place you hands behind the back of your head
4. Lift with your lower back until your body forms a straight line from toe to head.
5. Lower your body slowly
6. Repeat the exercise 10 times
7. Perform 3 sets of 10.

Special Note: consult with your family doctor if you have a history of back problems

# Breaks

The break is the part in your voice where the chords are as tight as they can possible be... they cannot vibrate any faster. So instead, they burst apart, and you lose all your tone quality.

You 'break' into falsetto and all of a sudden, your voice lacks power.

### How To Get Past The Dreaded 'Break'
As speech level singing taught me, it is possible to erase this break entirely. So much so, that a listener won't even notice when you pass through this area in your voice. It's like having different gears. You reach the 'breaking point', but instead of breaking, you move up a gear, and continue to sing higher.

This 'changing of gears' as I have called it is the point where your vocal chords form a new muscle coordination. This is called a 'shortened' vocal chord.

Meaning, a section of your vocal chord 'closes'.

This 'section' that is now closed, stops vibrating.

The part of the chords that is still vibrating is now shorter. This means it's easier for this shortened section to vibrate faster, making it MUCH easier to hit higher notes.

Identify the spot where your break is.

This might not necessarily be the same note every time, but it should be close to the same. Once identified, work on scale exercises that take you through your range and instead of waiting for the break, work on switching between the voices several notes before it. This will allow you to control the switch rather than just letting it switch naturally.

Your scale exercise will help you develop the muscle memory so that it becomes as natural as your breathing.

## Phrasing

Phrasing refers to the breaths or "stops" in-between notes. Natural phrasing will include "stops" after all periods, commas, semicolons, or colons.

Additional phrasing may be necessary for the singer to take catch breaths or to achieve a certain style. It's an excellent idea for singers to sit down with sheet music or lyric/lead sheets in hand and mark their phrasing before they begin to sing. This helps prevent unexpected losses of breath and awkward phrasing that draws attention to itself.

Listen (and try to imitate) singers like Frank Sinatra or Sammy Davis Jr. (for men) and Ella Fitzgerald or Anita O'Day (for women).

Their phrasing was so unique that it could transform a good song into greatness. Sinatra was noted for his unusual phrasing that often imitated the phrasing of the horns in the orchestra!

These singers are also noted for their mastery of breath control, essential for proper phrasing.

## Using Rubato

What does that mysterious Italian word Rubato mean? It means "stolen time" in English--and seems easy to explain, but really isn't. In the simplest terms, it means going behind and ahead of the meter in a piece so the piece becomes multi-dimensional rather than seeming deliberately mechanical. It also means slowing down and speeding up certain passages, which is basically the same thing as lagging behind or ahead of the beat.

Mind you, when people attempt to do it for the first time on an instrument or while singing (especially musicians used to strict counting on the beats)--they frequently get thrown off on the time or accompaniment.
It's something you have to either feel or mimic rather than a teacher sitting and explaining any kind of workable theory behind it. That's not to say that there aren't numerous books on the market that attempt to teach it to those who just don't have a clue how to demonstrate the technique. The only way to really learn it intuitively is to hear other pianists and singers demonstrate it.

It is often used in jazz and classical styles, but you will hear many examples of it in rock music as well.

Not surprisingly, Frank Sinatra was the pop world's master of Rubato!

Even Classical music lecturers will sometimes tell you to listen to Sinatra's recordings to understand Rubato in a way that makes more sense to modern audiences. In a way, Sinatra's sense of Rubato in a pop and jazz vocalist sense may be even more complicated and easy to throw you off. That's because the accompaniment with him is always a strict beat (Chopin's left hand)--but the vocal line can potentially dance around that steady rhythm.

30

You have to have a real profound understanding of the values of notes, where you're starting to rob the time...and where you'll ultimately end up so you don't sound like you're lost. Believe me, I've heard amateurs try to tackle Sinatra and Nelson Riddle's original arrangements--and they almost always get thrown off before even getting halfway through.

All of the other great pop singers of Sinatra's time didn't take as many chances with Rubato as Sinatra did. Frank was truly a masterful musician outside of anything else people have a beef with in his personal life. If you listen to other singers of his time--most of them play it safe compared to Sinatra's more dangerously Rubato-like performances on many of his classic recordings. The greatest aspect to that was seeing Sinatra live in concert. Because Frank made each musical line have its own give and take against the backing rhythm--it enabled the illusion you were hearing a different song each time he sang the song live. That's why you can hear those old bootlegged (or Sinatra family-approved) live recordings available on the market with the same old set lists--but feel like you're hearing a different concert from another live recording done around the same time period.

The only singer I've heard recently who's managed to pick up on that sense of Rubato successfully is Michael Buble. Most of his live recordings give you a chance to hear a fresh take on his hits every single time. Well, that makes sense, considering he studied Sinatra recordings--along with other singers of the time period. It also seems to prove my theory that you can learn Rubato by listening to others and having a subconsciously astute musical understanding.

## Open Throat Singing

Remember when you went to the doctor and he placed that wooden tongue stick on the back of your tongue and told you to say "AHHH!"

**That's Open Throat.**

To sing with Open Throat means to sing in the yawing sensation, the back of your throat should be open to help your voice go forward, to your natural resonant cavities. Your soft palate is going up giving you the sensation that the throat is open.

There are debates among vocal coaches as to the value and methodology of open throat singing, so it's important to remember that you should experiment with various techniques to find the one that's right for you.

**How do you know it's right?**

By the tone you eventually achieve.

When you yawn two things happen: your throat opens up and the soft palate lifts up creating more space which is what you need to make a good sound. The other thing that happens is the lungs fill up to the bottom. Once this has happened, tighten up your abs to control the flow of the air through your open throat. Keep your throat relaxed and keep concentrating on what you need to do until it becomes second nature.

**Constrictor / Tongue Relaxation Exercises And Tips**

1. Monitor your daily voice habits to keep vocal stress at a minimum.
--Never yell or scream, especially in noisy places. Even trying to speak loudly over noise can cause hoarseness. If you must raise your voice try to project using your lower body support muscles, without any pressure in the throat.

-- Try to speak in your "optimal pitch" several times a day, first when alone, and then when speaking to others. This speaking pitch usually differs from your usual or habitual pitch and is found this way:

Agree to something sincerely with an "um-hmm!" with your mouth closed. You might use a slight inflection (slightly higher than normal pitch). When you make this "agreeing" sound see if you can feel a gentle vibration in your nose and mouth area.

Now say something in a pitch close to this, again looking for that sensation in the nose and mouth area (the "mask"). You'll know it's correct if your throat feels free and relaxed in this pitch and your voice sounds more resonant. When practicing at home:

Say this: "um-hummm, Right!" "um-hmmm-- of course!" "um-hmmm-one" "um-hummm-two" and so on.

2. Relax your shoulders. With head held back comfortably (avoid this exercise if your have neck problems) let your jaw relax and drop open, your mouth open. Feel your tongue completely relax. Pretend you are sleeping on a couch with your mouth open (see illustration below).

Now pick your head back up and keep your mouth in this relaxed and open position for a few seconds, noting how relaxed it feels. In singing or speaking the jaw should always open back and down in this relaxed way, never force it down with your jaw muscles as this causes tension in the jaw and tongue. Instead when you open your jaw, think of releasing it.

3. Now with good posture place your hand on your chin and say "Yah, Yah, Yah", gently guiding your chin down with each syllable. Your tongue will relax and pull forward a bit. Practice saying "Yah-Yah" like this in different, yet comfortable speaking pitches, noticing how relaxed your jaw feels.

4. In front of a mirror relax and let your tongue stick out. Now on a sustained "ah" slide up and down in pitch a few notes like a siren sound. Do not do this in a very loud voice. At first your tongue may tighten on the way up. Try to practice until you can see and feel it relaxing. Next wag the tongue (still outside of your mouth) gently side to side while sliding up and down in pitch. Never force these exercises.

5. In front of a mirror say "ee-ah" several times with an open and relaxed jaw. Do this so that you only see your tongue move up and down inside of your mouth while the jaw does nothing. Speak or sing this exercise in low, medium and high pitch levels. You can start this by holding the jaw a bit with one hand.

6. Practice swallowing (constrictor muscles) and yawning to feel the difference. The swallowing muscles are the ones which close the throat. We need to relax these constrictors for singing. Good vocalizing occurs by using the released and relaxed yawning position with a relaxed tongue.

33

8. Try holding your nose and breathing in through your mouth. You should feel cool air slide over the back of your tongue if your throat is open. If your breath feels shallow it means that the root of your tongue is most likely blocking the air. Relax and try again.

The goal of every singer should be to achieve tonal balance. Many of the popular techniques that vocal teachers use to help their students improve the quality of their voices are devices for directly or indirectly enlarging and relaxing the throat during singing. The use of imagery, such as 'drinking in the breath', in their teaching is very common.

Enlarging the throat space involves conscious inhibition of some of the natural reflexes, such as the swallowing reflex, a condition that is nevertheless essential to good tone production.

There is no science to refute that the teaching of the open throat is good pedagogy. The intricate relationship of muscles in the throat is positively affected when the head is allowed to be free on the neck.

Each muscle achieves its proper length and connection with the others in an optimum state for functioning well. The muscles work together, each set meeting the opposing pull of the other, which allows the larynx to become poised, balanced and properly suspended.

The vocal folds are actively lengthened and stretched by this action, and thus brought closer together. In these favourable conditions, they can close properly to execute the sound quickly and efficiently, and thereby produce a clear, clean tone with a minimum amount of effort. The throat is then properly 'open'.

However, relying upon the open throat technique as the cure for all singing problems is potentially shortsighted and problematic, as a 'closed throat' neither causes nor explains all vocal issues.

# Hard Palate Resonance

**Mouth (Oral Cavity)**

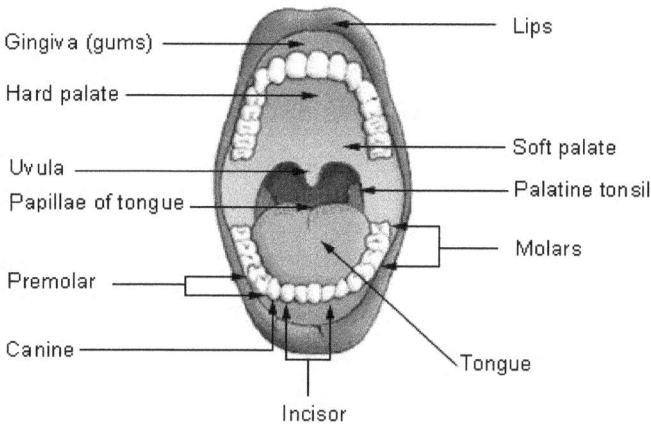

Gingiva (gums)

Hard palate

Uvula

Papillae of tongue

Premolar

Canine

Incisor

Lips

Soft palate

Palatine tonsil

Molars

Tongue

One technique I try to always use when singing is something I call "roof of mouth resonance," or "Hard Palate Resonance."

The palate refers to the roof of the mouth. It has two parts: the hard palate (the anterior roof of the mouth) and the soft palate (the anterior of the roof of the mouth). The hard palate is formed by the palatine process of the maxillae and the palatine bones' horizontal plates. A mucous membrane covers these bones. The ridges along the hard palate are formed by the palatal rugae (also called the transverse palatine folds) which are necessary as they allow the tongue to maintain its position through friction when a person swallows.

The hard palate is connected to the soft palate. It is found on the anterior region of the mouth, a soft muscular structure that is covered by a mucous membrane. Near the middle portion of the soft palate, a suspended extension called the palatine uvula can be found. When a person swallows, the soft palate and the uvula are pushed upward. This action is vital because it closes the nasopharynx and stops the food from being admitted into the airway. Two muscular folds called the plossopalatine arch (anterior) and the pharyngopalatine arch (posterior) can be found along the uvula. Between the two folds is the palatine tonsil.

Singing from the diaphragm, and keeping the throat fairly open, imagine the tone hitting the roof of your mouth (Hard Palate).

This will give you a visual reference when working with sound and tone, and can be very effective in voice control.

## Saving Your Voice

Think of your voice like a natural resource. If you use it efficiently, properly, it will last you a long time. If you waste it, treat it harshly, blow it out, it will fade sooner than normal. Worse, improper vocal habits can cause long term or irreparable damage.

Don't be among the singers who overuse their voices.

**How to Save Your Voice from Common Mistakes:**

**Oversinging:** This means singing too loudly, or for too long, using restrictive singing techniques like squeezing the throat, adding too much breath pressure or muscular force, screaming, yelling, singing through pain or discomfort. You can damage your voice beyond repair from these harsh techniques. Even a bit of oversinging, over time will affect the quality of your singing and reduce the longevity of your voice.

**Not Learning Vocal Technique Properly**: Some people are blessed with cognitive skills to learn to sing naturally, and have free vocal production and healthy technique on their own. If they pay attention to their voices, how they feel, how they change over time, they are lucky.

Some of us need the extra guidance of a reputable voice teacher. Someone who knows the craft of singing, the vocal anatomy, and can communicate effectively to a multitude of students with various problems. Working with a professional teacher, even from time to time, can be a valuable tool in addition to rigorous self-study.

**Singing the Wrong Music:** This has less to do with technique and more to do with artistry. If you are a tenor with a light sound, you may never sound like Bryn Terfel, the glorious booming baritone, or a bass will not be able to cover Led Zeppelin tunes, echoing Robert Plant's outrageous high pitched vocals.

Sing music appropriate for your voice type and skill level. In additional to lowering the chances of hurting yourself, your audience will appreciate music that is perfectly suited for your "instrument." You wouldn't hand out the wrong symphony parts, giving the trumpets the violin sections, the cellos the percussion part!

So does singing music you weren't meant to sing.

Take good care of your instrument.

**Tips**:

### 1. Pretend that you have a balloon in your stomach
Whether or not your beer belly is the size of a compact car, I still want you to learn how to do diaphragmatic breathing. It'll make everything else work and sound better. Put your hand on your bellybutton and when you breathe in through your nose try and fill up your stomach area as if there was a balloon in there. Then as you exhale let your stomach fall back in to its normal position.

When you breathe like that, it sends an even amount of air out of your mouth that the words can ride out on. When that happens you sound a lot more resonant and powerful, and the tone of the voice changes from nasal and harsh to warm and commanding. Most people miss the most important element of the breathing thing…you have to let your stomach come back in the whole time you're speaking. If you're not letting your stomach come back in, you're actually holding your breath.

Do you really think it's a good idea to do a three or four hour show holding your breath whenever you try to speak? Fix that and a lot of your voice problems will be history. Swallow without water, fine. If not, take a sip and then swallow. By the way, you won't need to be clearing your throat that much if you follow my advice and drink a half gallon of water a day and lose the coffee and the caffeine. That diet will make sure that you always have just the right amount of lubrication on your cords.

## 2. Only breathe in through your nose

There are little filters in your nose that purify and moisten the air that comes in that way. Every time you breathe in through your mouth, and most of you do, you're making your vocal cords dry and red. When they get really dry, you'll start to lose your voice. Do a little experiment for me right now. Take a big breath of air in through your open mouth. Do you feel how that makes the back part of your throat feel dry? Now, take a big breath in through your nose. Do you notice how that doesn't make the back part of your throat feel dry? Keep practicing that and remind yourself during the off air breaks.

## 3. Drink at least a half gallon of water a day. I know that most of you would rather drown than drink regular water all day long. But water is the number one way to keep your vocal cords in great shape. The cords are basically slamming into each another hundreds if not thousands of times a second when you speak. And all of that is happening while air is being blown at them. That's why they get dry so fast. You can't just drink water and expect that to go right to the cords and make it all better.

When you drink, the water actually goes down a different hole in the back part of your throat and doesn't even go near the cords. The only way to get the water to the cords is to drink so much of it that the blood stream carries brings it to them. To make that happen you need at least a half gallon a day.

When I say water, I don't mean the water that's in coffee or tea or soft drinks. I mean plain ordinary water. When you think about it, drinking water is really not that much of a price to pay to keep your voice in great shape.

## 4. Avoid excess coffee, tea and caffeine. When your mom brought you hot tea with honey and lemon to comfort you when you had a sore throat, she was obviously trying to help. If you're still drinking that daily now, you need to make some changes.

Here's why:

The tea is too hot and it can make your vocal cords change size, even though they live down another hole in your throat. Haven't you ever looked at your hands after you get out of a really hot bath? You don't want to make your vocal cords look like prunes, that's not going to help your show.

Caffeine speeds up the production of extra thick phlegm. When your phlegm gets too thick you end up having to try and clear your voice all the time. I'd rather you spend more time talking and less time choking on junk that shouldn't be in your throat.

Lemon and any other citrus makes you salivate more. When you salivate that end up creating the extra thick phlegm you don't want.

**Stop Clearing Your Throat Like a Bulldozer.** You need to stop trying to clear your throat by making the same horrible sound as the monster from 10,000 Leagues Under The Sea. All you're doing is making your vocal cords more red and swollen. There really is no way to effectively get rid of the excess phlegm at that moment. All you're doing is actually moving the phlegm from one place on the cords to another; you're not getting rid of it at all.

The best advice I can give you is to simply swallow. That moves the phlegm around without hurting the cords. If you can, swallow without water, fine. If not, take a sip and then swallow. By the way, you won't need to be clearing your throat that much if you follow my advice and drink a half gallon of water a day and lose the coffee and the caffeine. That diet will make sure that you always have just the right amount of lubrication on your cords.

### 5. Beware of Headphones
You might think that the headphones are your best friend but that's just not the case. You're getting ready for the show, you're all psyched up, you put the headphones on and hear a voice that is suddenly loud, powerful, resonant, commanding and bassy. You feel bigger than life and ready to save the world. There is, however, one big problem, what you're hearing has absolutely nothing to do with what your listeners actually hear coming out of their radios.

The headphones create a false sense of what your voice actually sounds like. Once your sound enters the microphone it's shaped and colored by all kinds of electronics. That's why you need to make adjustments based on what you sound like in the room before it goes into the Mic.

The easiest way to do that is to have one side of the earphones fully on, and the other side slightly off your ear. Then, you need to concentrate on the sound that's coming out of your mouth, right in front of you, instead of focusing on the sound of your voice in the earphone. It might take a little practice but it'll be worth it when you understand that you have to make your voice sound the way you want, and not rely on the electronics to do for you.

If you really love having both earphones on, and you feel that you just can't hear the guests, or whatever when you have one partially off…use my technique to practice before you go on the air. Make your voice sound the way you want, and then don't change anything when you put both of the earphones back in place.

**6. Stop Whispering.** The worst thing you can do is whisper. As a matter of fact, whispering is harder on the cords than screaming. The reason is, when you whisper or speak too airy, extra air passes through the vocal cords and dries them up. When the vocal cords get dry, they get red and swollen, and that's how you get hoarse.

If you have a sexy airy quality to your voice and that's your signature style, you still need to find a balance between how much edge (pure sound) you have, and how much air. Most people also think that if they speak really breathy and airy on air that all of that sound will get to the listener.

The truth is however, there's only so much of that airy sound that gets picked up by the Mic, the rest dissipates before it ever gets to the listener. So, try to pay attention to whether or not you have too much of the airy/whispery sound in your voice. If you do, say the word, "Brat", and hold out the "a" sound like this, "Baaaaaaaaaaaaaaaaaat." The buzz you feel when you hold out the "a" is what I mean when I say edge. You'll need to add a little of that sound back into your voice.

**7. Practice Before you Preach**. No professional runner would ever run the race before they stretched. If they did, they would just pull muscles and shorten their careers. What makes you think that you can just open up your mouth and have incredible sounds come out without doing any warm up?

I believe that speaking doesn't effectively warm up the voice at all. You need a few minutes of vocal exercises that'll make the cords move effortlessly all the way up and down the vocal range. That's the only way to get the consistency you long for.

If you warm up daily, you'll be able to count on the fact that your voice will be there when you want and need it. Otherwise it's always going to be the luck of the draw. I recommend that you purchase warm up exercise tapes and use it in the car on the way to the studio. It'll be a great gift to give yourself.

**8. What To Do if You Get Hoarse**. If you're drinking the amount of water I recommend, not whispering, not smoking (you thought I'd forgotten about that one), not clearing your throat like a moose in heat, breathing in through your nose, cutting back on the caffeine, and warming up your voice with a few good vocal exercises, you're well on your way to having a much healthier voice.

If something happens and you do get hoarse, I suggest you learn to speak like Yogi Bear. That's right, as if you weren't already enough of a cartoon character, making that sound will actually help you lose the hoarseness.

Put your finger on your Adams apple and say the word, "No". Now add that funny Yogi Bear/ Sylvester Stallone in Rocky bassy quality.

Did you feel your Adams apple come down lower in your throat?

This is called a "Low Larynx Sound," and helps to reduce the swelling of the vocal cords. If you play around with that for a few minutes, or do the Low Larynx exercises on my warm up tapes, it'll take care of the hoarse problem and get you ready to go back on the air in minutes instead of days.

# II. PROBLEMS AND SOLUTIONS

## THE 10 MOST COMMON PROBLEMS OF SINGERS

In dealing with the physical production of the singing voice, one encounters many problems, all of which are interrelated, and often addressed simultaneously. The ten problems listed below are prevalent in different types of singers, regardless of training and experience.

**1. POOR POSTURE:** The efficient alignment of the body is of primary importance to voice production. Problems in posture range from "collapse" of the chest and rib cage, with corresponding downward "fall" of the head and neck, to the hyper-extended, "stiff" posture of some singers, that results in tension throughout the entire body. Effective posture evolves from the kinesthetic awareness, that may be developed through the study of a physical discipline such as Hatha yoga or Alexander Technique.

**2. POOR BREATHING AND INAPPROPRIATE BREATH SUPPORT:** Some beginning voice students seem to "gasp" for air, and exhibit clavicular or shallow breathing patterns. Trained singers, on the other hand, use primarily diaphragmatic breath support. The muscles of the lower back and abdomen are consciously engaged, in conjunction with lowering of the diaphragm. As the breath stream is utilized for phonation, there should be little tension in the larynx itself. Sometimes, in an attempt to increase loudness (projection), a well-trained singer may over- support or "push" the airstream. This extra effort may affect vocal quality by producing undesirable harmonics.

**3. HARD GLOTTAL OR "ASPIRATE" ATTACK:** "Attack" or "onset" (a preferable term for singers) occurs with the initiation of phonation. Some singers (possibly related to poor speech habits) use a glottal attack, which is too hard (produced by to much tension in closure, hyper adduction. Vocal cord nodules may develop with habitual use of a hard glottal attack. The opposite problem is the "aspirate" attack, in which excessive air is released prior to phonation. While this type of attack rarely damages the vocal cords, it causes a breathy tone quality. (This technique may, however, be utilized to help correct a hard glottal attack).

**4. POOR TONE QUALITY:** Many terms are commonly used to describe a singer's tone, and among those familiar to singers are: clear, rich, resonant, bright, . . . dark, rough, thin, breathy, and nasal. Although, "good tone" is highly subjective, according to the type of singing and personal preference of the listener, in general, a tone that is "clear" (without extra "noise") and "resonant" (abundant in harmonic partials) is acknowledged as "healthy" and naturally will have sufficient intensity for projection without electric amplification.

Opera singers strive to develop a "ring" (acoustic resonance at 2,500-3,000 Hz), that enables the voice to project over a full orchestra, even in a large hall. However, for other styles of singing, the use of amplification may allow a singer the choice of employing a less acoustically efficient vocal tone for reasons of artistic expression. A breathy tone, for example, may be perceived by the listener as "intimate" or "sexy", and even a "rough" sound, such as was used by Louis Armstrong (false vocal cord voice), may represent a the unique persona of a performer.

**5. LIMITED PITCH RANGE, DIFFICULTY IN REGISTER TRANSITION:** All singing voices exhibit an optimal pitch range. Typically, untrained voices have narrower pitch range than trained singers, due to lack of "register" development. The term "register" is used to describe a series of tones that are produced by similar mechanical gestures of vocal fold vibration, glottal and pharyngeal shape, and related air pressure. Some common designations of registers are the "head" register, "chest" register, "falsetto", etc.

Singing requires transitions from one register to another; each of these transitions is called a "passaggio" ("passageway"). Lack of coordination of the laryngeal musculature with the breath support may result in a "register break", or obvious shift from one tone quality to another. Untrained male voices and female "belters" tend to "break" into falsetto/head voice in the upper range. Regardless of the style of singing, a "blend", or smooth transition between the registers is desirable.

**6. LACK OF FLEXIBILITY, AGILITY, EASE OF PRODUCTION, ENDURANCE**: Traditional voice training in the 18th-19th century "bel canto" ("beautiful singing") method places emphasis on vocal flexibility or agility -- for example, the singer's ability to execute rapid scales and arpeggios. Virtuosic technique demands excellent aural conceptual ability, coordination of an abundant airstream with energetic diaphragmatic support (sometimes perceived as "pulsations of the epigastrium"), and clear, resonant tone quality. The use of rapid melodic passages in vocal training helps to develop a relaxed, yet vital voice production, that contributes to the development of increased vocal endurance.

**7. POOR ARTICULATION:** Pronunciation with excessive tension in the jaw, lips, palate, etc., adversely affects the tonal production of the voice. Problems of articulation also occur when singers carry certain speech habits into singing.

The longer duration of vowel sounds in singing necessitates modification of pronunciation; the increased "opening" of certain vowels in the high soprano voice, or elongation of the first vowel in a diphthong, are examples. Retroflex and velar consonants (such as the American "r" and "l") need careful modification to allow sufficient pharyngeal opening for best resonance, and the over anticipation of nasal consonants ("m", "n", "ng") may result in a "stiff" soft palate and unpleasant tone.

**8. LACK OF DISCIPLINE, COMMITMENT, COMPLIANCE**: As any athlete knows, regular practice is essential for optimal development and performance. Unfortunately, the need for disciplined training is not always apparent to singers. Furthermore, "artistic temperament" may contribute to a lack of compliance with the advice of teachers on issues of vocal technical development. When a teacher's advice is contrary to a singer's own established ideas and work habits, the singer may tend to overwork, overperform, or simply "try too hard" in practice. The singer's practice and performance regimen must be sensible, productive, and acceptable to both teacher and student alike.

**9. POOR HEALTH, HYGIENE, VOCAL ABUSE:** Many students ignore common sense and good vocal hygiene. The physical demands of singing necessitate optimal health, beginning with adequate est, aerobic exercise, a moderate diet (and alcohol consumption), and absolute avoidance of smoking.

College voice students often test the limits of their vocal health by overindulgence in "partying", alcohol or drugs, and by screaming at sports events. Many singers are careful with their voices but abuse their voice by employing poor speaking technique (see, for example, Bogart-Bacall Syndrome in this issue).

Professional singers who travel are frequently confronted with changes in their sleep and eating patterns. (Specifically, singers should avoid talking excessively on airplanes that are both noisy and dry).

Performing in dry, dusty concert halls, or singing over the din in smoke-filled clubs increases the risk of vocal fatigue and infection. A minor cold or allergy can be devastating to a professional singer, who is obliged to perform with swollen (edematous) vocal cords. Good vocal hygiene, good travel habits, and vigilant protection of ones instrument (good judgment) is an important responsibility of every singer.

**10. POOR SELF-IMAGE, LACK OF CONFIDENCE:** Although many singers appear to have "healthy egos" and may display the aggressive behavior that is known as "prima donna" temperament, such behavior is a cover-up for anxiety and/or insecurity. Since the slightest aberration - phlegm, for example - can result in momentary loss of voice (even in the greatest of performers!), singers often feel that they are always in a state of vulnerability. Despite unpredictability in vocal performance, the singer does gain confidence through repeated performance and increased self awareness.

## Other Problems To Consider:

## Pitch
Even professional singers experience pitching problems. Every singer sings off pitch sometimes, but some singers continually struggle to sing the right notes. They do not have the ability to sing 'by ear', and

they can't pretend to get the hang of matching their voice to a specific pitch.

Several singers who have pitch problems blame tone deafness, but this is really very rare. If you have pitch problems, they are probably the effect of one of these common issues:

## Instrument Problems

If you sing or plan to learn to sing with a band or play your own musical instrument while singing, incorrect tuning can affect your pitch. You might think you're singing the right note, but you're basing your pitch on incorrect tuning. Use a tuning device or strike a note on a piano to be sure your instrument is precise.

Volume is another issue that can interfere with your ability to stay on pitch. If the guitar and piano are too low, or if the bass or electric instruments are very loud, you might have problems hitting the right notes.

Typically vocalists cannot hear themselves during live performances. This can be disorienting and can cause pitch troubles. If you suspect this is the reason for your off-pitch singing, use good quality in-ear monitors when you sing live.

## Recognizing Notes

Some people can determine notes simply by hearing them once. This is called 'perfect pitch,' and it's rare. Most of us need to hear the notes many times before we can fit their pitch.

Start by playing a scale on a piano or guitar. Actually listen to the notes and how they resonate. Play through the range several times, and then play through while matching your voice to the notes.

It's simple to let your mind wander when you do this form of exercise, but try to stay focused on the notes. Pay attention to how your throat feels when you hit each note. With enough practice, you'll be able to keep on pitch even when you can't hear yourself singing.

# Physical Barriers

Vocal chord stress and chronic health difficulties can make it difficult to sing on pitch. To cure this, you'll need to address and treat the root cause of the problem.

Sinus infections, colds, and allergies can leave you with a stuffy head that makes it hard to discern pitches, much less sing on pitch. If you're suffering from an illness, give yourself and your vocal chords time to rest and recover.

Tension can also keep you from staying on pitch. Loosen up your vocal chords by warming up thoroughly before you sing. Do stretches to loosen up your other muscle groups at the same time. Stand up tall when you sing to give your lungs room to enlarge.

## Pitch Problem Solutions

Once you've found out the cause of your pitch trouble and you want to continue to learn to sing, you can take actions to fix it. If it's just a few instrument tuning and volume, it must be a quick fix. Get a tuning device to help you get your instruments on the correct pitch, or adjust the volume as necessary.

Record your voice when you sing along with different notes played on an accurately tuned guitar or piano. Play back the recording to determine which notes need more work. After a week or so, you will hear a significant difference in how well your voice fits the notes.

## Colds

When I first started playing gigs professionally, as a singing drummer in a travelling road band, colds used to wipe me out and prevent me from singing at all.

The bandleader and lead vocalist, who was classically trained, never seemed to be affected by colds. He always sang the same, no matter how sick he was.

When I asked him about it, he said "I sing through the cold. The secret is in the diaphragm. If you sing from the diaphragm and keep the throat open, you can sing through it."

Well, yes and no. Because the nasal cavity is the resonator, you still won't get the same tone, and it won't be pleasant trying to hear your self and resonate properly, but the end result can be just as pleasing even though you yourself may not be able to hear it.

It took me many years to master the art of singing through a cold, but it can be done. And since a professional singer can't call in sick, they must learn to sing through colds and flu and all sorts of sinus and throat infections.

But beware, if your vocal cords are inflamed with laryngitis, or you are hoarse, do not attempt to sing or you can damage your voice, and sometimes permanently.

Mark Baxter, a leading vocal coach, as this to say about singing with a cold:

*Winter and show biz don't mix. Biting winds and piles of snow keep potential audiences at home and make things difficult for load-ins. Then there's the additional burden of protecting your voice while everyone around is coughing and sneezing. As a singer, you can't afford to succumb to the average two colds a year. Even if you're a trouper and refuse to cancel, your instrument will be compromised and susceptible to harm. Not to panic, injury to the vocal folds is reversible, but taking time off to recover will put the brakes on your band's momentum. Prevention is the answer. The good news is, for every cold-forming scenario, there is a counter measure. The bad news is, by the time the first symptoms show, it's too late.*

*The germs which cause colds are always around. Constantly washing your hands and avoiding contact with others is not enough. The best defense is to keep your immune system strong by eating right (fruits and vegies), hydrating (two liters of water per day), sleeping (around six hours), and exercising for better circulation. Staying warm is also an important factor. In frigid conditions, your body works hard to retain heat. Dressing in layers, with a hat, water-proof boots and a scarf allows your body to focus energy on fighting off incoming infections. Use your brains. Wait until you stop sweating before going outside after rehearsal, and, leave a coat stage-side if a club requires a load-out directly after the set.*

*The winter holidays are a notorious time for coming down with something. Heavier foods and less physical activity increases the amount of toxins in our system. After a while, our bodies will clean house by producing mucus. So, find a way to stay physically active between Thanksgiving and Christmas -- and watch that third piece of pie. However, an abrupt change in lifestyle can also bring on a similar cleanse reaction. People who quit smoking cold-turkey or dramatically change their diet can expect cold-like symptoms to follow. I don't want to discourage anyone from becoming healthier, merely suggesting a gradual change if you've decided to clean up as a New Year's resolution.*

*Stress, of all the causes of illness, is number one. Juggling work or school with rehearsals and gigs, eating on the run with zero sleep, disrupts metabolism and forces the body to run on adrenaline. Anxiety saps vitamins, dehydrates, and leaves you vulnerable to whatever is around. That's why colds always arrive right as your preparing for the big recording or showcase. Yes, you should be well rehearsed, but there comes a point where the push becomes counter-productive. Rest, like hydration, is an inseparable component of vocal ability. It's important to remember that stress is 100 percent internal, and is always reduced by saying the word, "no." So, for your voice's sake, open up your schedule -- and chill.*

*I know it's seems uncool to worry about health, but ask anyone who has toured for a length of time -- getting sick on the road sucks. It is not inevitable that you will catch a cold every winter. Hold firm to a belief that you will not get sick. If it's too late for this season, then for next. Adopting healthy habits now will pay off in spades in the future when you're in demand. There is no remedy as effective as prevention. I'm sure your mother already told you most of these things, but that was so you wouldn't miss school. I'm telling you so you won't miss a gig. Big difference.*

*Okay, now let's pretend that, despite your best efforts, you've come down with a nasty, aching, head clogging cold three days before an important gig. Is there anything you can do besides crack open a bottle of Jack Daniel's? The answer is yes, but they aren't nearly as much fun. To minimize the effect a cold has on the voice you've got to act quickly. Keep in mind that congestion, mucus, is what your body produces to flush out toxins. Over-the-counter medications (anti-histamines) dry up congestion but prohibit the necessary house cleaning. They also dry mucous membranes, like your vocal folds, which will cause you to lose your voice. So, reach for the decongestants as an absolute last resort. However, it is better to experiment with medications at rehearsals, rather then waiting until gig day. You should always know the effect something will have on your voice before you use it under the spotlights.*

*If you have time, instead of squashing the symptoms, help speed up the cleanse. Flood yourself with water and real juices to thin the congestion, lubricate your folds and flush your body. The juice should be freshly squeezed in order to get the most benefit. The best types during a cold are Orange (vitamin C), Celery (retains fluids), Cucumber & Cranberry (cleans acid deposits) and Carrot (vitamin A). If you're not into juices, take supplements. The water-based vitamins like C and B complex are the first to be depleted when you're fighting a cold. Unfortunately, a Mountain-Dew slushy has no vitamins, but does give a great brain freeze.*

*An important benefit of hydrating is that it may keep a cold from reaching your lungs. Throat clearing and coughing, which normally accompanies a cold, is very irritating to the vocal folds. The delicate membranes in and around the larynx become swollen and rigid, which is why your voice gets so deep and restricted. Inhaling steam will help loosen congestion in the lungs as well as soothe the vocal folds. Be careful when inhaling steam, you can burn your lips and nasal passages. Gargling with warm salt water will also help draw phlegm away from your larynx. (If the salt is collecting at the bottom of the glass, you've put in too much.) This is a good routine to get into daily, to clean and increase circulation of the mouth and throat. Teas, honey, or any other coating therapy may soothe soar muscles but will not heal the vocal folds. To reduce the swelling and get singing again, you've got to vocalize (warm up).*

*Low volume, barely audible, humming is a great way to start. Let your larynx choose the pitches. It's better to stay with one single note (whichever is most comfortable) than to push or force the range. Allow plenty of time for your voice to loosen. Rushing the warm-up when you have a cold will greatly reduce the longevity of your voice and make conditions worse the next day. I once did a ten hour warm-up for a forty minute set. Refer to the warm up routine in lesson three, but remember, it's not what you're singing to warm up, it's how.*

*Sleep as much as you can during the days leading up to your performance, even if that means skipping rehearsals. But, on gig day, don't hibernate. Get up, take a long hot shower and do some light stretching and exercising to get your blood circulating. Mentally prepare for the long day ahead. Yes, it would be much easier to numb yourself with a bottle of Jack, but your condition the next morning will be twice as bad. The bottom line is, if you want a career as a performer, you're going to have to learn to sing with a cold. Might as well start now.*

Which leads us to…

## Hoarseness

The treatment of hoarseness depends on the cause. Many common causes of hoarseness can be treated simply by resting the voice or modifying how it is used. An otolaryngologist may make some recommendations about voice use behavior, refer the patient to other voice team members, and in some instances recommend surgery if a lesion, such as a polyp, is identified. Not smoking and avoiding secondhand smoke is recommended to all patients. Drinking fluids and taking medications to thin out the mucus may help.

**How to prevent hoarseness**

Specialists in speech/language pathology (voice therapists) are trained to assist patients in behavior modification to help eliminate some voice disorders. Patients who have developed bad habits, such as smoking or overusing their voice by yelling and screaming, benefit most from this conservative approach. The speech/language pathologist may teach patients to alter their methods of speech production to improve the sound of the voice and to resolve problems, such as vocal nodules. When a patient's problem is specifically related to singing, a singing teacher may help to improve the patients' singing techniques.

**Prevention tips:**

•If you smoke, quit.
•Avoid agents that dehydrate the body, such as alcohol and caffeine.
•Avoid secondhand smoke.
•Stay hydrated—drink plenty of water.
•Humidify your home.
•Watch your diet—avoid spicy foods.
•Try not to use your voice too long or too loudly.
•Use a microphone if possible in situations where you need to project your voice.
•Seek professional voice training.
•Avoid speaking or singing when your voice is injured or hoarse.

## Sore Throats

If you are sick with a sore throat, go easy. If you must sing, as in, you have a gig and you can't cancel it, then you have to be careful you don't make your vocal cords even more irritated than they already are.

A little warm up is good, keep the vocal cords moist and keep yourself hydrated.

Many people ask whether it is safe to sing with a sore throat. Depending on what's causing it, singing with a sore throat can be catastrophic. Experts suggest, "if it hurts to swallow, don't sing!" Conversely, if it's a mildly soar throat (due to cough or other reasons), consult your doctor (it's a good idea to find a good ear, nose, throat specialist in your area and build a relationship with him) and then use your best judgment.

Dry air, singing abusively, and viral/bacterial infection are some of the more common causes of a sore throat. Some people just wake up with a sore throat every day of their life. I've found that the majority of those people have acid-reflux, which means they are burping up stomach acids while they are sleeping or sometimes even while they are awake. For most, however, this happens in the night, so they may be completely unaware of the problem. They then wake up with a scratchy, raspy voice and a sore throat.

**Remedy :** A dry throat is often a sore throat, consume two to three quarts of water every day. If you live in an arid climate, sleep with a humidifier next to your bed and try to warm up your voice in the shower. The moisture is an incredible help for your voice. Also, learn to breathe in through your nose as much as possible. This will help moisten the air before it reaches your vocal cords.

When the unfortunate happens and damage to your vocal chords is done by singing with a sore throat, there are a few things that can be done to help repair the damage. You should never have to suffer through pain and irritation after a performance. But if you do, try drinking herbal tea to help coat the lining of your throat, softening the tissue around the vocal chords. Also, there are voice exercises and breathing techniques that can be done to help soothe and strengthen the voice box.

### If Your Voice is Straining, Ease Off

Whatever you do, don't strain to hit high notes in order to give a better performance. It isn't necessary to damage your vocal chords on your way to being a better quality singer. After all, you've worked hard and practiced with a passion in your quest to finding your voice so why undo all that work? And keep in mind that preventing a sore throat is always better than singing with one!

## Losing Your Voice - Laryngitis

When you lose your voice, you may have what is medically called laryngitis. If you can't talk or if you feel like you're straining your voice when you speak, you may be coming down with a cold.

However, there are other illnesses and conditions that may be the cause. Too much talking or raising of the voice, excessive smoking, or coughing all cause the vocal cords to become inflamed. Sometimes laryngitis can be a sign of a more serious condition that requires professional help.

If you lose your voice or experience difficulty talking, consult with your doctor to rule out any serious disease such as cancer. When consulting with your health care practitioner, you may want to ask if you can treat your condition yourself by using the following methods:

1. Give your vocal chords a rest. Overworking your vocal chords will only make matters worse. Abuse of this kind can very well be the reason you lost your voice. Try not to verbally communicate with anyone unless absolutely necessary until you can speak again without feeling like you're straining your voice.

2. Keep the larynx and the surrounding area well hydrated. Drink plenty of tea with honey and other fluids. Thyme or chamomile tea should bring some relief. Don't take in caffeine or anything that may cause dehydration.

3. Use a humidifier. Moisture in the air will help keep your vocal cords hydrated.

4. Avoid smoking cigarettes, and avoid being around smoke and other irritants you shouldn't inhale.

5. Take showers and breath a little deeper. The steam will help keep your vocal chords moist.

# III. VOCAL EXCERCISES

## Vocal Warm Ups

The first technique to be used in doing a warm up for singing has a variety of names such as buzz, bubble lips, lip roll, or lip trill. This is done by exhaling through puckered lips, thus creating a vibration. This may sound like a motorboat or a "raspberry".

Practice doing the buzz slide in between three tones. These are the base tone, up a fourth, and back to the base (do-fa-do): in the key of C major, it would be C,F,C. Continue with a half step each tone. C#, F#, C#, then D,G,D, then Eb, Ab, Eb, etc. you can also use the syllable "ee" or "oo", with the buzz enables you to make use of good breath support.

You will do the buzz slide between three tones: the base tone, up a fourth, and back to the base (do-fa-do): in the key of C major, it would be C,F,C. Repeat, moving up a half step each time (C#, F#, C#, then D,G,D, then Eb, Ab, Eb, etc.). You can also do this on the syllable "ee" or "oo", but the buzz forces you to use good breath support.

Next step is the fifth-slide. Begin the fifth note with "wee" and glide down to the base such as so – do: in C major again, it would be G, C. Do it again on the same tone, this time using "zoo", afterwards, move half-step higher and repeat the "wee" and "zoo" on Ab and Db. Keep moving up half-step each.

The next warm up for singing is known as the five-tone descending scale. This is done by taking up first on the fifth tone, then, descend stepwise towards the base: so, fa , mi, re, do. Use the syllable "na" first, then do with "nay", "noh", and "noo". Rise half-step higher and repeat the whole scale using every syllable.

The fourth is the descending 8-tone scale (do, ti, la, so, fa, mi, re, do) with the syllable "noo". As previously done with the other exercises, move up half-step then repeat. Test other vowels like "nah", "nay", "nee", or "noh", or "m" instead of "n" as its consonant. Sense the mask vibrating in your face or on your upper resonance while doing this.

Support this by following with a descending arpeggio: do, so, mi, do, on the syllable "nah". Repeat using "nay", "nee", "noh", and "noo", after which move up by half step and repeat once more each syllable.

Finally, the octave slide. Utilize the buzz and start with the basic note. Then slide up an octave and slide down again towards the base: do, do, do. Repeat with the syllable "oo". Then, move half-step higher again with the buzz then the "oo".

The final warm up for singing is the octave slide. Use the buzz and start on the base note; slide up an octave and back down to the base: do, do, do. Repeat on "oo". Move up a half-step, do the buzz, and then "oo". Keep doing this by moving up half-step.

Voice exercises are designed to help improve your singing and to develop quality voice and build vocal endurance and agility. You are doing the wrong thing if you strain your voice. If that is the case, simply stop the routine. Singing must be done in a relaxed manner, even if you are hitting the high and powerful notes. Good vocal exercises help manage your voice and keep it able to perform. Here are some of the most common exercises that help to keep your voice in good shape.

## Proper Posture

The first step before jumping into the proper singing exercise is to maintain the proper posture. Keep the chin level, head up, knees loose, and shoulders relaxed. Keep the abdominal muscles and back muscles relaxed and make sure the toes are pointed forward with your weight placed on your heels and not on your toes.

## Breathing Exercise

Take a deep breath and hold it to the count of five, then exhale to the count of five. Then do the same routine ten times. To increase the level of breathing inhale again, but this time, you create a "sshh" sound when you exhale. Do this routine five times.

## Motor Boat Exercise

Getting the idea from the word itself, you mimic the sound produced by a motor boat. It is very simple, just put your lips together then exhale while you are making your lips flap. Start projecting the sound in a lower voice then increase to move to the higher notes. The target aim of the motor boat exercise is to loosen the vocal cords and train the vocal muscles.

## Pick a Note

This exercise aims to hold the note for longer periods of time until you perfectly hit the correct note. Just simply sing do, re, me, fa, so, la, te, do, over and over again. Use various mouth shapes to enunciate well each vowel ( "ee", "a", "aah", and "ooh")

## Diction Exercise

This time, you can sing a song phrase to improve diction or you may try these good examples below:

" Do, re, me, fa, so, la, te , do"( going up the scale)
" La, lo, le, lo"
" Ta, to, te, to"
" Hi, he, ha, ho, hu"
" Fluppy floppy puppy"
" Sally saw silvester stacking silver saucers side by side"

## Cool Down Exercise

In every rigid activity, a warm-up exercise is necessary. What most singers do not realize is the importance of a cool down exercise to calm down the blood flow to the larynx. In some cases, the larynx is most likely to swell if the calm down exercise does not happen. How do you do the cool down exercise? Just hum a song at a very relaxed pace. Easy, simple, and should never be taken for granted.

## Record the Practices

The best way to monitor your progress is by recording all your practices. You can immediately spot the areas which have a need for improvement and areas you are having some difficulties in. Remember, whether you are just singing in the church, community, or school, you have to ready your vocal cords for a strenuous activity before anything else

Vocal exercises to improve singing are very important and can really help with some of the areas that you may need to improve. So knowing how to do the vocal exercises correctly seems to be the problem that most beginners are having difficulty with.

The rule of the thumb: Always begin with a warm up exercise before jumping to vocal exercises. So that way, you can stretch your voice in preparation for more rigid vocal training. To give you an idea, here are some of the most common warm-up exercises in singing.

Humming warm-up – just say the ward "hmm" and allow the pitch to slide upward while saying it, and as the pitch goes higher, feel the buzzing sensation in the nasal area. Now, let the pitch slide down while saying the same word and feel the buzzing sensation resonating in the chest area.

Lip trill – known as "bubble" because of the same sound we produce, "brbrbrbrbr" when we submerge our face under water. This warm up builds up a healthy and strong voice. While producing bubble sounds, do not blow the air from the mouth by pursuing the lips. To do the exercise correctly, place one of your fingers on each hand to each side of the face and push into your cheeks.

Then, gently push your cheeks while pushing your fingers outward in order to support the lip muscle. If you're unable to produce "brbrbrbrbr", you can try to move on and produce one note with your voice while still doing the lip trill exercise.

Scale Singing – this is a very good exercise to warm up your voice and learn the basics in scale which are very essential to keep you in the right pitch while singing. The Major Scale is very common, as we all know the basics of Doh Re Mi Fa Sol La Ti. The Doh is added in the highest octave in continuance of the Ti scale.

Always start with the lowest note before working out your way to the highest scale. The most ideal for men is to begin in B major scale, while A flat major scale for the female counterpart. The reasonable explanation would be the adjustment of vocal cords and needs to adjust for lower tension before it could be stretched out for a higher scale.

These three warm up exercises are enough before we can jump into much more rigid vocal exercises. It is also worth taking a note that after the proper vocal exercises, cool down exercises should not be taken for granted. The simplest way to do it is by soothing the vocal cords with the descending scales on the "ee" or "oo" vowel sound.

What are the consequences if the singers that do not subject to cool down exercise? Imagine that the vocal tension will remain tensed and will eventually lead to voice complications. So, in order to maintain a healthy singing voice, essential warm up exercises and cool down exercises should be put in the primary and last on the singer's inventory.

If you want to make the most of your voice and have an even sound and tone from the top of your range all the way down to your lower notes then these daily exercises will help you achieve this goal.

Keep a look out for my other articles on how to prepare for singing and breathing exercises which will follow and try them before doing the sets below.

## Steps

1) Say "le" and "la" out loud and try to use an Italian accent (say "le" instead of "lay-ee" and "la" rather than "la-uh"

2) Join the vowels "a" and "e" together with the "L" in a curving arc type sound flicking your tongue quickly making the "L" sound as short as possible.

3) Do this exercise for a few minutes

4) Say with an Italian accent vowels a, e, i, o, u, prefixed with the lip consonant "m"

5) Pronounce these vowels in sounds in the following way: "ma" for the "a" vowel as in the name Arthur. "me" as in the "e" in wheel. "Mi" as in machine. "mo" as in the "o" in more and "mu" as in the word "tool"

6) In order to produce the correct sound required for the "m" sound, spring open your lips and this will help pronounce the sound and project the note out

7) Ensure throughout the exercise maintain a good focus on good quality consistent breathing

## Extra Tips

In singing Italian vowels are almost always used in singing so it is important in learning and practicing this way of letter pronunciation.

Also by improving your pronunciation of the following consonants (L, M, P, T, D, F, G, N, S, V, Z) this will work towards good exercising for your tongue. For example, as opposed to using the whole length of your tongue to produce the sound "L" practice just using the tip of your tongue curled backwards. It actually makes it easier to say in fact.

## Steps

1) If you take the melody of a song that is familiar to you can replace the lyrics with the Italian vowels from the above exercise for a good workout and practice.

2) The method is called vocalizing and to illustrate look at the following example: Somewhere over the rainbow / Way up high / There's a land that I heard of / Once in a lullaby / Somewhere over the rainbow / Skies are blue / And the dreams that you dare to dream / Really do come true.

3) Using a steady flow of breath use should vocalize this example focusing on the "la" and "ma" sounds

4) Memorize all the lyrics to the song you have been practicing with the Italian vowels then sing the actual song with the lyrics.

5) Instead of looking at the written lyrics try looking outwards and sing as if you are looking at an audience watching you perform.

## Final Tip

When you listen to your favorite songs try not to copy the voice of the singer but rather see it as your own version of the song when you sing it. It may be fun to copy your favorite pop star but if you mean to do singing as a profession it best to do it your way in order to not damage the vocal system and also help bring out your own potential.

## Cooling Down

After a singing session, the singer should cool down the voice with exercises that soothe the vocal cords such as soft descending scales on the "oo" or the "ee" vowel. If the singer does not cool down after a sing session, the vocal tension will stay and the vocal cords remain tensed and this will lead to further voice complications. So, to maintain and preserve a healthy singing voice, adequate warm up and cool down is a must in any singer's inventory.

## Scales - Are They Old Hat?

**No! Scales may seem old fashioned, but they *work*.**

You also need to sing scales more often than normal if you have pitch problems. Most coaches will recommend 20-30 minutes a day when starting out.

Practicing scales will also strengthen the muscles used for singing and give you better control. To practice scales, identify your range (tenor, baritone, soprano, alto, etc.) and know how to find the notes that cover your range on a keyboard or piano.

Then practice the major scale in every key moving up and down using the vowel sounds. At some point you can start working in minor scales as well. Solfege (Do,Re,Mi,...) is also an effective tool for improving pitch problems.

There are innovative ways to vary your scales, but the main scale you will be working with in the chromatic scale.

The chromatic scale is a musical scale with twelve notes, set a semi-tone or half step apart. These twelve notes, or tones, in the chromatic scale represent all of the notes in Western music.

Singers often work with the chromatic scale to exercise their voices because singing the chromatic scale offers a vocal challenge. Singing the chromatic scale effectively teaches singers to hear, and sing, smaller variations in pitch. The exercises a singer can do with the chromatic scale are almost endless, and each variation offers special challenges.

**Tools and Training**
Most singers will not be able to perform the chromatic scale or any of the scale variations without first gaining some margin of ear training. One way to train the ear, and the voice, to the chromatic scale is to play every key on the piano and sing along. Start with an octave your voice is comfortable with and work up or down from there. Stop when you can no longer comfortably sing a note or when the you cannot match a tone. Software is another ear-training option. Solfege is free ear training software for PC and Mac (see resources) that allows singers to utilize the entire chromatic scale in a variety of exercises designed to train the ear and the voice to recognize tones and semi-tones.

**Chromatic Scale Vocal Runs**
Use the entire chromatic scale to perform expansive vocal runs. This is a difficult challenge for all but the most accomplished singers, but practicing such runs can develop the voice quickly and effectively. Expansive vocal runs using the chromatic scale require singers to begin on one note of the chromatic scale and sing every note in ascending and descending order, including all sharps and flats as well as the octave, seeking to achieve a smooth transition between each note.

## Arpeggio Vocal Chord Progressions

Singing arpeggios in common chord progressions is an effective method that helps develop control of the voice as well as the ability to hear tonal variations and musical progressions. An arpeggio is a broken chord; a chord progression is movement between chords in specific keys. Singers often practice singing chords built from the chromatic scale based on common chord progressions.

There are numerous chord progressions possible, so you may want to purchase a basic music theory book to keep on hand while you practice. You can find one at a music or book store, or online at no charge. In addition to common chord progressions, you can practice singing chords built on every, or every other, note in the chromatic scale in consecutive order. This is difficult to master, but can effectively develop extreme vocal control.

# IV. LEARNING NEW SONGS

## Imitation vs. Innovation

While learning to sing, imitating the singers you are trying to emulate can be a richly rewarding learning experience. It is the best way to learn phrasing, breath control, pitch and tone.

But there comes a point at which the vocal techniques have been mastered in a song and the singer must find their own voice - their own interpretation of the lyric.

Once you have mastered the art of imitation, then comes the time when you must innovate. In that innovation you will find within yourself the voice that is uniquely yours.

## How do you find your own voice?

It is as individual as you are, for no two persons are going to sound exactly alike. The way you phrase, enunciate and the passion and feeling with which you deliver a lyric will always be yours and yours alone. It comes with practice, and it comes in the doing.

## Budding artists of all types face this difficulty.

Many writers and painters learn their craft emulating the great masters, and finally arrive at a point of jumping off where they spread their own wings and fly.

When I first learn a song, it's a frustrating experience. Once I learn the melody and write out the notes on the piano, then I sing it over and over again, just like the original artist recorded it, with all the same phrasing and nuances.

Once I learn the song, I put away the lyric and lead sheet and rehearse the song on my own, usually to a backing track of some sort.

What happens at first is that it's uncomfortable; the song often feels like it's not working with me singing it. I try to suspend judgment and criticism but I'm terribly self-conscious about it and I stuff towels under the door of my practice room.

It often takes my singing the song many times before I'm comfortable with it, and it never really becomes "my own" until I've performed it live at least a hundred times.

At that point, the song has become second nature, I no longer am self-conscious, and I am free to interpret it in a multitude of ways.

For jazz standards, I stay true to the original melody, but much like a jazz musician, I will often vary it, and improvise.

## Mark's Easy Song Learning Method - How I Learned The 'Crooners' Show

While learning songs for the off-Broadway musical review "Crooners," I used my own tried-and-true songlearning method. Since I don't read music and must learn songs by ear, I first started by typing out the lyrics to the song.

Then I would go through the song and listen to the original recording and make notations on the lead sheet. I've developed my own shorthand method for notes that sustain, and I place comma's between breaths and phrasing.

I'll draw in arching lines for bending notes and slides, as well as for stops and rests. I've come up with quite a few of these little shorthand notes.

I encourage you as a singer to develop your own shorthand notations for these various singing elements, so that you will instantly recognize them when you are practicing to your own lead sheets.

Once the notations are done, then I will "run" or listen to the song several times just going through it to become familiar with the melody, and as I do this, I am very quietly singing lines or words along with the original singer and keeping an ear out for my own notes to try and match them as closely as possible.

Often I will need to stop and write out difficult passages by finding each individual note on a piano, and then I will write each note over the lyric syllable the note falls on.

This can take quite a while, sometimes several hours for just one song, but once I do it, it's done, and I then have an instant reference for later when I am memorizing the melody and I get stuck.

Most pop or country songs for me are easy enough that I can remember melody without writing out the notes, but jazz and pop standards from the Great American Songbook are tricky songs melodically to pick up by ear, no matter how easy they may sound.

Even great pop songs that sound like bubblegum ditties on their surfaces can turn into amazingly complicated learning experiences. I discovered this when I once mistakenly thought I could learn many of the classic Beach Boys hits in short order for a show I was doing.

Think again!

The genius of Brian Wilson was not lost on me ever again after that!

## Memorizing Lyrics - Lose the Stand

Once I get the song down comfortably, I'll then lie down with the song lyric and memorize it. As a live performer, you should always strive for learning the song and memorizing the lyric so you will not require a music stand on stage.

A true professional singer, in my view, does not need the crutch of a music stand on stage. I know that as a singer I can never deliver a song the way I should if I have to read it off of a sheet.

Some may argue that other musicians read sheet music onstage, but those musicians aren't the focal point of a live performance and often back the lead vocalist.

# Don't rely on crutches!

Lose music the stand!

Memorizing lyrics for me is simply a matter of repeating a verse until I can recite it without looking, line by line, then looking back to the lyric to get the next verse, then putting those two together and so on until the entire song can be repeated without using the lyric sheet.

At that point, I will then rehearse the song to a backing track and put it all together.

If you are not used to memorizing lyrics, it can be difficult at first, but with time and practice you'll find memorizing songs becomes easier and easier. k

There's something in the way the brain works that when you exercise certain abilities, such as memorizing lines and song lyrics, that it becomes easier with time.

Thank God for that!

## Practicing - What, When and For How Long?

Depending on your professional goals, I generally recommend at least 30-60 minutes of practice per day, in addition to your warm up and cool down exercises.

It is a good idea to vocalize each day, keep the vocal cords limber, and keep the juices flowing.

I try to always be learning new material first, and then review the next most recent songs I've learned, and lastly, review older material to keep it fresh.

Mixing styles of music is also extremely helpful in developing your versatility as a singer, and allows you to mix and match vocal styles from each genre for a more unique approach.

# V. LIVE PERFORMANCE - TIPS AND TECHNIQUES

## Style

What is the music you most enjoy listening to? Chances are it's the same style of music you enjoy singing the most. If you like all styles of music, you may find your voice is more suited to a particular style.

You may be attending classes or doing workshops in one style, such as Broadway, and find it might not suit your taste, which could run to country-western or rock and roll.

It's important to like the music you are singing. If you are singing a particular style simply to get a job as a singer, and have no affinity for the style, you'll never be able to deliver the passion and conviction needed to pull it off, let alone the patience and dedication needed to master the style. (Unless you are a very good actor.)

## Experiment

For myself, back in my teens I started off singing hard rock. Then I joined a travelling road band that did Top 40. Later on I joined a Dance Music group singing Disco. And still later I began singing in an Elvis Tribute show, portraying King himself!

Today I sing a variety of styles, depending on the show I am working, but you may want to start by specializing in one particular genre, the one that speaks to you the loudest: the one that gets your furnace burning.

## Finding Your Voice

It's not always easy to find your own unique voice, the thing that sets you apart from other singers. It might take years for you to finally arrive at a "sound" that is so unique, it places you in a place that distinguishes you from the pack.

Often singers will make the mistake of imitating the latest trend or style of singing, only to find that style goes out of favor, and they are lost until they can either find their own voice - or imitate the next big thing.

While there is nothing wrong with imitation, as often it is required to work gigs, and as mentioned earlier, it's a wonderful way to learn the craft. But at some point you will be well advised to try and establish a sound and style that all your own, one that when a person hears your voice, they will know it sounds like no-one else.

## Getting Inside the Song - Making It Yours

How do you get inside of a song - to make it uniquely your own? First you must learn it - how you proceed from there is up to you.

I always listen to other singers and their own interpretations of the song, if it is available with jazz standards, there are often many versions of the same song, and I like to hear them all before going at it alone.

What is the emotion of the lyric? What is the songwriter trying to convey, it's essential meaning, and how can you get inside of the song and make it yours, to own it? For only once you own the song can you expect to be able to interpret it in a way that is going to be felt by your audience.

A song does not necessarily need to be sung well, technically, but it should be sung with passion, conviction and emotion; above all, with an HONESTY that makes an audience feel that emotion vicariously.

Emotion means conveying the meaning of a lyric in an accessible, honest way, with passion and feeling. Not overdone feeling, such as an amateur actor might over-act a scene, but with a sense of conviction that this particular set of circumstances is happening to you - and you are relaying that feeling in real and genuine way.

69

# Emoting: What To Do While You're Singing

This means quite possibly using your hands, your gestures, your expression all toward conveying that sense and meaning - and this often involves not standing completely still.

There are times when a singer's style *is* to stand completely still - there are no hard and fast rules, but my own particular style, at least when not playing guitar while singing a lyric, is to move around the stage, never staying still, in constant motion.

Watch how professional singers move, how they convey a lyric. Note what actions and performance techniques they use to move an audience.

When you watch a great master, you will see an economy of movement that is graceful and smooth, as the old saying goes they "make it look easy." Frank Sinatra was one of these kinds of singers, but there were many more.

Who could ever forget the heart-stopping gyrations of Elvis, or the amazing dance moves of James Brown or Micheal Jackson as they sang.

Ella Fitzgerald was another singer who could accomplish amazing feats of vocal prowess while connecting to her audience - and there were times when she barely moved a muscle!

Concersely, Mahalia Jackson was one of the most passionate and demonstrative  singers who ever lived. To watch one of her performances is to witness passion and feeling at it's most inspirational.

## Audience Awareness - Connecting is Important

I remember my first gig when I was just starting out singing as a professional lead vocalist, and I was scared out of my wits. Through the whole performance there was a spotlight in my eyes blinding me to the audience (which was probably a good thing) but it did little to blind me to my terror.

For the most part I sang almost the whole performance with my eyes closed, but didn't realize it till afterwards, when an audience member pointed out to me "Why did you have your eyes closed? Sing to the audience, make eye contact!"

Well, I never forgot that bit of advice.

The point is that vocalists can get so hung up on themselves and their technique they forget to make eye contact with their audience. Many times it's a reaction based on fear, or simply being self-conscious.

Always make eye contact with your audience, even if you are on a stage and follow spot is blinding you - pretend you can see them.

Scan the audience slowly and deliberately, the eyes are the windows to the soul.

Don't shut them out, they are your paying audience!

## Hearing Yourself: Monitoring Considerations

The toughest challenge any singer faces onstage is hearing themselves sing. With the band playing right next to you and a non-isolated drummer flailing away, it can become next to impossible to hear yourself sing, let alone get a decent "mix" of instruments relative to the vocals.

This is made even more difficult in situations requiring that vocalists harmonize with one another while backing musicians are playing.

Traditionally, speaker cabinets known as stage monitors or "wedges" placed on the floor in front of each musician and singer were the only way to get any kind of "foldback" from the mixing board.

Today the situation has improved dramatically with systems known as "in-ears" - small earphones or earbuds which isolate outside sound and allow only the mix the singer needs through.

Monitoring systems such as these can be complex and very expensive - with the better quality ones involving custom ear impressions and wireless transmitters costing into the thousands of dollars.

Depending on how far along you are in your singing career, you may want to invest in such a system - but beware that they can not only be expensive, but they can take some getting used to. Many singers find the isolation they feel when singing with in-ears in their ears very disconcerting - especially if concessions are not made to add an "ambient" mic of the audience to the overall mix.

With some tweaking, experimenting and the proper mix, using in-ears onstage can help save your voice from the screaming and yelling that often occurs when singers try to "compensate" for not being able to hear themselves over standard outside floor monitors.

For the rest of us, it's the war of the floor wedges - and the battle for hearing what you need to hear to sing properly - while still trying to protect your hearing - is on!

To learn more about in-ear monitors visit:

http://ultimateears.com/

# VI. IN THE STUDIO - TIPS AND TECHNIQUES

## Preparation

Like any professional, when it's game time, you are expected to perform and deliver results. Whether it's an indie recording project of your own or you are a gun for hire on someone else's project, be on time and be prepared.

Know your material inside and out, be rehearsed, warmed up, and ready to "kick ass."

Time is money, and recording studio time is expensive. If you are fumbling with words, spending time doing vocal warm up exercises, or making dumb mistakes, you are going to gain a reputation as being undependable, and will lose the respect of your fellow workmates.

Recording brings with it a pressure unlike any live performance. When the tape is rolling and the red light is on, it's like trying to perform in the Olympics.

Some say that being a professional is not just being able to deliver excellence anytime, anywhere, but also to be able to do it under immense pressure.

Give yourself the best advantage you can by knowing your material inside and out, be fully prepared and rehearsed.

## Windscreens

Studio microphones are incredibly sensitive and can pick up the smallest breath, noise, vibration, and.... pops.

Known as "plosives," the consonants like "P's" that create a massive pop sound when you sing can ruin an otherwise perfect take.

Using a windscreen on the mic, or pop-screen can help eliminate this.

## Pacing Yourself

Recording studio sessions often involve many takes of a single line or section of a song. Each repeated take can lose something of the original passion of the performance, and extensive takes can not only lack feeling, but can leave your voice strained.

Pace yourself through the session. Don't oversing, use your voice sparingly, and if it seems like the performance is suffering, reschedule the session or take a break.

## Playback and Monitoring

Make sure your headphones are delivering a decent mix that's not too loud, and one that isn't too heavily laden with effects. Some studios are equipped with a small mixer box right at the vocal microphone that allows the singer to adjust his own levels.

## Ear Fatigue

Too much time in the studio listening to repeated playbacks during recording and mixing can result in what is known as "Ear Fatigue."

The literal translation is 'tired ears.' Ear Fatigue is not really a clinically recognized state, but audio professionals have been referring to it for years. It's caused by a combination of TTS (Temporary Threshold Shift) and general fatigue.

The condition we call ear fatigue usually occurs after many hours of listening to or working with audio, especially when working at relatively high SPL's. It causes us to not hear the sound in the same way we do when we are fresh. Sometimes people report soreness of the ears associated with this, but not always. There are ongoing studies of this phenomenon, and the phenomenon of fatigue and how it affects performance in general, but much remains unknown.

Suffice to say that making critical audio decisions while in a fatigued state is not advised and generally results in doing the work over again. It's difficult to judge anything objectively when ear fatigue sets in. Your best bet in a case like this is to take a break, or reschedule the session.

## Pitch Correction

A process whereby the pitch of a selected track or part can be changed (or corrected) without changing the speed at which it occurs. A crude ability to do this has been around for some time, but only in recent years has the technology reached a level where it's practical and easy to apply. One of the first devices to come out that made this possible was the old Eventide Harmonizer , a device designed for generating harmony parts. By today's standards it didn't work all that well due to the fact that formants were also shifted in pitch, which gives you the Mickey Mouse or Darth Vader effect depending on whether you are moving the pitch up or down. And for pitch correction it was entirely a manual process that was a bit hit or miss in terms of quality. Later, devices (including more sophisticated Eventide units) and software arrived that could handle formants separately, which allowed users to create much more realistic harmony effects.

Though the sound was much better actually correcting pitch problems in a track was still largely a manual process that could take hours. Over the years technology has improved to a point where software and/or hardware can now correct the pitch of a whole track (or live performance) automatically just by knowing the key and tuning of the song.

If applied sensibly there are so few side effects that listeners can't tell the performance has been treated electronically.

Singers today can have their flat or sharp vocals digitally corrected in the studio, but beware if you are relying too much on this device, for it is not a real and accurate representation of your voice when you sing live.

If you are having pitch problems, you are well advised to get the problem straightened out in the early stages of your career as a singer, for sooner or later the rubber must meet the road and you must perform your vocals before a live audience, who will know if you are sharp or flat.

## Harmonizers

These devices were originally trademarked by Eventide to describe their range of products that have pitch manipulation capabilities. In the early days of the company they were actually called Eventide Clockworks, which had to do with what some of the founders' "day gigs" were.

Back in 1975 they came out with their first Harmonizer (the H910). It had the ability to pitch shift audio in realtime (actually there were a few milliseconds of delay involved) up or down one octave. The product was a huge hit in studios and live sound, where it was used as much for doubling (simulating the sound of a double track) as actual pitch transposition. This is mostly due to the fact that the resulting quality of the transposed pitch was not very true to the sound of the original track as there were many digital artifacts created in the process, not to mention the resulting Darth Vader or Mickey Mouse effect caused mostly by transposing formants along with the pitch.

For a doubling effect it sounding pretty good - distinctly different from the delays and choruses that had commonly been used before - and became a bit of a trademark sound in the late 1970's. The rest is history.

Eventide continued to build better and more sophisticated Harmonizers over the years and even though many of their features and concepts have been effectively copied their products remain on the cutting edge and their status in pro audio history is legendary. It should be noted that even though many people use the word Harmonizer as a generic term to denote any box that can effectively pitch shift audio in realtime Eventide guards this trademark very closely.

# VII. PSYCHOLOGY

## Criticism

The criticism that can come from even your friends and family once you decide to become a singer can be devastating. While support is always helpful in any endeavor, remember in the arts you must walk your own path, and not be affected by the opinions of others, good or bad.

Even pop idols are not unaffected when it comes to criticism, and each must deal with it in their own way. Some simply refuse to read reviews or criticism of their work, or read articles published in the press.

**How to deal with criticism**
Criticism is something that every single musician will be subjected to in one form or another whether you want to or not, so here are some thoughts on how to make the most of criticism. These ideas should work for any musician, regardless of genre or instrument.

**To accept it or not**
The first thing you need to remember is that not all criticism is justified or valid. If you're standing in front of your teacher in class, or if you're at work playing in a band or orchestra, then it's likely that some good points are being brought up and you should probably pay attention.

If the person criticizing you is a friend or someone just randomly stopping you to tell you what they think about your singing, it is possible that they are doing it out of envy or just to cut you down.

Not worrying too much about what others think is one thing. Making yourself blind to things that could help you is a different thing altogether.

**Separate yourself from your Singing**
Some people just can't give critique in a good way, even if the critique itself is justified. They might have excellent points to make, they just can't make them in a way that isn't offensive and mean.

So to avoid feeling like you've just been axed in the ankles, you need to learn how to interpret any kind of critique in a constructive way, regardless of how it was expressed. This will take some practice and getting used to, but believe me, it's an incredibly useful skill to have.

So how does one accomplish this? One way is to learn how to separate "you" from "the result of your work".

Just be patient and don't take it personally.

In the music business, as in life, don't take anything too personally.

Do your best, put it out there, and don't agonize.

One last tip: Always make sure you are as prepared as you can possibly be for every single performance. There is no such thing as a performance too small to take seriously, so either be sure to perform as well as you can every single time, or don't accept the job in the first place.

Of course, this doesn't mean that you won't sometimes get criticized anyway. There will always be people who have something to say about your performance, and that's perfectly normal. Don't be afraid of criticism. Just see it for what it is and use it to your advantage instead!

## Self-Confidence

**"A musician must make music, an artist must paint, a poet must write, if he is to be ultimately at peace with himself. What a man can be, he must be." -Abraham Maslow**

Maslow's quote above illuminates a very important point. Many of us in our rush to fulfill the obligations that others have set out for us, fail to point ourselves in the direction of the thing that is most vital and integral to our identity. When that happens, we become miserable. And if you are reading this right now, you most likely identify some part of yourself as that of a singer – or at least you want to be.

Singers come in all shapes and sizes across a vastly wide arc of development that spans from the shyest, fresh seemingly incapable beginner, to the most vibrant and wildly emotional and advanced vocalist. Wherever you are on the spectrum doesn't matter. If you are reading this article, chances are, you feel the seeds of a singer somewhere in the seat of your individuality. The fact will remain the same – you ARE a singer.

You have a right and an obligation to fully become your potential. If you didn't have that right, you wouldn't feel the urge you feel to become it. Not everyone will be a Whitney Houston or Freddie Mercury, but they have already existed anyway, so no one would care all that much even if you were their incarnation. We've already had them. But if you are drawn to singing, whatever becomes of your interest in singing, fame or fortune are irrelevant. What matters is that you sing – because that is your bliss, and that is a part of who you are.

The challenge with all art is to master the craft, and weave your personal identity through it. It involves a triple ongoing life process of working with a mentor you trust, identifying and learning from your heroes, and learning about your identity. The rest inevitably works itself out as it should.

Let's explore this idea of safety and self-esteem further – but I'm going to come at it sideways. Have you heard about the 7 year old prodigy painter Kieron Williamson in England?

At seven years old, he is already being compared to Picasso. Instinctively sensing his own greatness, he swore to his parents that he would be very good at something – he just didn't know what it would be. After trying a few different things, he found painting. His parents, a former electrician and a nutritional therapist with no artistic ability between them thought it was a phase:

"He was passionate about trains when he was little and that passed. Then it was dinosaurs and that passed. This artwork thing he's stuck at for 18 months. He asks questions Keith and I wouldn't have a clue about, the difference between watercolors, oil and pastel technique. We put him in touch with artists who can answer his questions. Other than that and a six-month local workshop in 2009, Kierson has taught himself shading, depth, proportion and coloring in three media. Once school resumes next Tuesday, he'll revert to his old painting hours: "I paint in the morning until half past eight and from half past three in the afternoon. Four or five hours a day."

For some reason, as singers, very few of us receive this kind of support from our surroundings – so we often get a bit of a detour around what we love. But even more importantly, we pick up lots of dialogue that works completely against ourselves, trapping us into shame about what makes us blissful, and locking up our voices metaphorically, and physically.

We normally have 2 voices in our head: The free child-like creative flow, just like the story above, that loves to find new relationships, meanings and experiences. The "child" knows no limits, only boundless potential.

Moving through life's continual stream of roadblocks is acceptable, exciting, and routine. But then we have the critic – the voice that takes it all apart, and makes us rational – sometimes violently. Both have their purpose, but the critic can be deadly in the early stages of raw, tender but fertile creative development.

We love to bludgeon ourselves with negative criticisms: "I'm not gifted enough/not clever enough/not original enough/not young enough". Pick one – or all. They come easy don't they? Self, meet your critic.

The following exercise will seem silly and redundant, but I implore you to try it anyway. There's a profound gem in it, especially for us as singers. I've borrowed it from Julia Cameron's famous book "The Artists Way".

Pick an affirmation. Get out a piece of paper and a pen (no typing), and write this down on it: "I, (your name), am a brilliant and prolific singer".

Did the ears of your censor perk up yet? What did it say? Write down what the critic said on the bottom.

Continue to write the same affirmation above again on paper: "I, (your name), am a brilliant and prolific singer" – except this time, write it 10 times. And stay alert.

Something amazing will happen. Your censor will begin to object – probably many times. Objections will fall out everywhere. You will be amazed at the rotten things teething under such a harmless exercise. Write them down. Write them ALL down as they come to you in your writing of the affirmation. In their nasty claws lies the psychological freedom of your vocal potential and creativity.

Become a detective. Where did those blurts come from? Scan your past… Was it something someone said? Mom? Dad? Sister? Once you put your finger on the monsters originations, you can start to work with it.

Counter it with your own affirmations that give it equal measure in a supportive direction. These are your own, unique personal affirmations – and nobody has to see them but you. It may feel awkward at first, but if you use your new affirmations regularly, daily, you will sow new artistic seeds, change your outlook, and put yourself firmly on the path to your true potential.

This exercise is immensely revealing (and healing), if you can get over the seeming embarrassment of having to say good things to yourself. But you have to choose wisely what tapes you want to play in your mind. One leads to misery, the other to your bliss.

Do we really say all these things to ourselves? Yes, I believe the vast majority of us do. Critical thinking is vital to our survival as animals, but murder to our fragile creativity, especially as singers where we are so dependent upon the healthy exuberance of our nervous systems.

Only when the nervous system is optimally prime, can our voices be in a state of balance. When it's not, the voice is the first thing to go. As a singer, having a psychologically balanced state of mind will allow you the emotional endurance for the often long road to developing technical mastery.

Our throat is the potentially blissful creative valve that turns the air we breath, into the sound that marks and gives us our unique expression. But it is also a tender soft spot where we can be silenced and/or dramatically inhibited, so incredibly easily.

When we tell ourselves how bad we are/how much we don't deserve it/that we'll never amount to anything, our nervous systems responds obligingly through and into our throats in all kinds of nasty and unwanted ways. Whatever we tell ourselves we are, is what becomes of our biology.

But what if you were to wake tomorrow and have no memory of the negative criticisms you've accumulated, and the only sense you had was of your own boundless potential for the thing you loved – your voice?

That would change everything wouldn't it? You would MAKE time to practice your singing because having no right reason to deny it to yourself – you find yourself free to dazzle in it, like the child above.

Put the critic in it's place – he/she has no right to overcrowd and kill your fertile space. Don't get caught in a terrible self-inflicted story that keeps you creatively stuck and trapped in fear. Re-write the story. As a singer, you are providing the soundtrack to people's lives – even if only at karaoke. Be open. Be creative. Be a conduit. Allow yourself to just *be*.

You can claim your potential as a singer. Of course it takes time. It's an art like any other, and everyone's path will be different. As long as you keep learning, the very act of being in the process of becoming will provide you with enough excitement and new discoveries to keep you moving steadily towards your goals. But you have to stop talking bad about yourself TO yourself in order that can give yourself the chance to allow your unique voice to truly blossom.

## Ego

Many eastern spiritual texts put forward the idea that you must learn to have a full awareness of your whole self. While our self looks like it is an integrated whole from one level, scratch the surface (via meditation or other methods of self-enquiry) and you will find a whole heap of different parts of your personality, all striving to express themselves.

The one that stands out the most initially is the Ego, the self-important, self-centric aspect of our personality . The ego (which is a modern western psychological term I might add) has been given a fairly bad rap in the modern "new age" scene.

Somewhere along the way, our Western minds have turned this into the ridiculous notion that to be happy you must get rid of, or even completely destroy the ego.

My own personal experience has brought me to a different understanding. I believe that there is no reason to destroy what is essentially a part of yourself. The real power is in learning to integrate this and all of the other interesting and unique parts of your personality into a functioning whole.

People go through life without a second thought to the idea that there are separate parts of their self, which manifest themselves at different times and in different situations. The ego is just one of these parts, the one that thinks that it is separate from the rest of creation, and that IT is the most important thing in the known Universe.

And quite frankly, it is good to have this instinct kick in from time to time. It stops you getting walked all over, gives you the confidence to claim your place in the world and also to create and express yourself. Knowing that YOU are you, what your place in the world is has a profound importance to our whole selves. But it also has a negative side of selfishness, aggressive behavior and helping us justify doing things that may not always work out best for everybody involved.

The image that makes the concepts more tangible for me is the Yin-Yang. Your personality is in constant flux, and each part must be in harmony with the other for balance.

The Ego, or separate, selfish self must be brought into balance with your quiet, inner, calm, connected observer self. Let one part express itself too much and you become overbearing, self-important and obtuse. Too much of the other and you become meek, mild and can have no meaningful interaction with the outside world.

Hey, and don't get too beat up if you find yourself acting like a complete fool from time to time. Seriously, everyone does it!

DYNAMIC balance means that even though you may find yourself at one end of the Ego scale, you have the self awareness to bring yourself down to a centered state at the appropriate time.

Of course it is not as clear cut as all that, and these are only arbitrary labels that we have placed on very strange and complex phenomena. But at least it gives you a framework to get our talking monkey-brains around and be able to see where all of the pieces fit in.

So in order to address this all important balance, here are my top 5 strategies to keep your ego in proportion.

1. Realize your size in proportion to the universe
When it comes down to it, you are a tiny speck on a tiny speck, floating in a vast sea of nothing more giant and unfathomable then you could ever get your head around. The very notion that what you do on a daily basis affects things at the scales that really seem to matter in the universe is wishful thinking gone crazy. As Seamus put it in his excellent "Looking through the wrong end of the telescope": You. Don't. Know. Anything. About. Anything.

The liberation and true freedom of insignificance is yours to grasp at any time. When the ego gets up and starts jumping up and down about its importance, just keep this fact in mind to bring it all back to perspective.

2. Realize that you are where you are only through the help of others
The network of other people you build up around you in friends, co-workers, family and neighbors is one of the most fundamental assets in life. Think that you have accomplished so much in your life? Sure, a lot was done by you, but there is no way anyone could get anything done without the help, co-operation and support of people around them. All of life is a team exercise.

3. Understand that everyone is just as important as you

A lot of the ego's jumping up and down, complaining and self importance is because it believes it is more important than ANYONE else in the world. You know why so many people in traffic jams start getting irate and honking their horns? It is because each of those people think their journey is more important than the person in front of them. Next time you feel the anger and indignation that the ego fires up when it feels like it is being threatened, just remind yourself that everyone, and everything is just as important as you in the universe. No more, and no less.

4. Realize the inherent impermanence in all things

As I stated before in the "Impermanence Top 40", today's front page news is tomorrow's forgotten fact. So many events in our life that the Ego blows up into monumental proportions seem trivial the next day, and are forgotten next week. Nothing lasts forever, and nothing remains in the same state as it is now for even a second. Strive for your goals, and enjoy the journey. But Realize that everything is just a castle in the sand, to be washed out to sea by the waves of time.

5.  Realize that humor is the true currency of the universe.

Just about anything in life has a funny side to it, when looked at from a certain perspective. The greatest way to disarm the Ego is to see the inherent humour in everything. When we laugh, we see the connectedness of things, the joy in everyday life and Realize that the world is not such a serious place after all.

Humor is all about connectedness, it shows us how previously unthought-of concepts are connected in unexpected ways. It connects us to others in the shared experience of having a laugh and goofing off for a while.

Next time you find yourself acting from ego, have a laugh.

# VII. CARE OF THE VOICE

1. Maintain Good Posture and Proper Breathing Control When Singing

Always make sure that we maintain an upright and neutral posture and practice proper breath support when we sing! practice these basic breathing exercises in order to establish better breath control in our singing. If we wish to, there are also other more advanced breathing exercises that we can practice in order to be more proficient in our breathing control!

2. Practice Vocal Warmups Before We Sing

We should always be sure to warm up our voices before we start to sing, so that our diaphragm and our vocal cords are ready to support and produce the sound that we require during singing. Check out some useful vocal warmup exercises in order to achieve better voice care and protect our singing voice.

3. Regular Exercise and Proper Diet

This point applies to our voice care and also to our bodies in general. Achieving a good level of personal health is certainly beneficial to maintaining a great singing voice. This is because when our bodies fall ill, we may feel fatigue, experience blocked noses, sore throats or may not even practice proper vocal technique when singing. This will cause unnecessary damage to our voices, and we would do well to keep ourselves healthy so that our voices will be healthy too!

4. Keep Our Neck, Jaw and Face Relaxed During Singing

When we sing, we control our breath using our diaphragm and the surrounding abdominal and intercostal muscles, and our voices with our vocal cords and supporting muscles. We should always take care not to involve other muscle groups into the picture, for example our neck muscles, jaw muscles and facial muscles. These muscles should be relaxed when we sing, as they will affect our voice by increasing the amount of tension in our throats and in our vocal cords, and making it more difficult for us to sing well!

Understand more about some common singing problems by clicking on this link, and you will know how to overcome these problems with some simple tips as well as constant effort on our part!

5. Placing or Focusing Our Voice Appropriately

- There are a great variety of vocal registers and positions that we can sing from, and knowing which register to use as well as which position our voice should resonate from will be beneficial to general voice care and avoiding vocal damage. For example, we would not wish to place a very high note in too low a position, or to use a low register to stretch and reach for a high note! Do check out the rest of this website for more information on vocal registers as well as positions!

6. Reduce Speaking Time in Noisy Environments

When in extremely noisy environments, for example at a busy construction site or at a crowded club or pub, we would find that the overall noise level in these places are far higher than what we usually encounter in our daily lives. As such, when we try to speak in these noisy conditions, we cause a lot of strain on our voices and may hurt our vocal cords in the process. Reducing our speaking time in these noisy environments will help to avoid unnecessary damage and aid in protecting our singing voice!

There are also some specific guidelines regarding usage of medications that we would do best to bear in mind:

1. Avoid anti-histamines, decongestants and anti-depressants. These tend to cause dryness in our voice and make it difficult for us to sing well, as our vocal cords need to be well hydrated and moist in order to function properly.

2. Avoid over-the-counter local anesthetic medication for the throat. These tend to reduce nerve sensitivity in our throat and also create numbness, making our voice more susceptible to damage. In a sense, it is something like driving when we are blindfolded, as we are unable to feel our voice or our throat sensations and we do not know if we abuse our voices or employ too much of our throat muscles to sing!

3. Take antacids for acid reflux. Acid reflux causes acidic fluids to flow back up towards our throat and may hurt our throat tissue as well as our vocal cords! Learning to take care of our acid reflux problem will certainly help to keep our voices healthy and free from damage!

4. Avoid alcohol.

5. Don't smoke!

## Tips to Prevent Voice Problems

- Limit your intake of drinks that include alcohol or caffeine. These act as diuretics (substances that increase urination) and cause the body to lose water. This loss of fluids dries out the voice. Alcohol also irritates the mucous membranes that line the throat.

- Drink plenty of water. Six to eight glasses a day is recommended.

- Don't smoke and avoid second-hand smoke. Cancer of the vocal folds is seen most often in individuals who smoke.

- Practice good breathing techniques when singing or talking. It is important to support your voice with deep breaths from the diaphragm, the wall that separates your chest and abdomen. Singers and speakers are often taught exercises that improve this breath control. Talking from the throat, without supporting breath, puts a great strain on the voice.

- Avoid eating spicy foods. Spicy foods can cause stomach acid to move into the throat or esophagus (reflux).

- Use a humidifier in your home. This is especially important in winter or in dry climates. Thirty percent humidity is recommended.

- Try not to overuse your voice. Avoid speaking or singing when your voice is hoarse.

- Wash your hands often to prevent colds and flu.

- Include plenty of whole grains, fruits, and vegetables in your diet. These foods contain vitamins A, E, and C. They also help keep the mucus membranes that line the throat healthy.

- Do not cradle the phone when talking. Cradling the phone between the head and shoulder for extended periods of time can cause muscle tension in the neck.

- Exercise regularly. Exercise increases stamina and muscle tone. This helps provide good posture and breathing, which are necessary for proper speaking.

- Get enough rest. Physical fatigue has a negative effect on voice.

- Avoid talking in noisy places. Trying to talk above noise causes strain on the voice.

- Avoid mouthwash or gargles that contain alcohol or irritating chemicals. If you still wish to use a mouthwash that contains alcohol, limit your use to oral rinsing. If gargling is necessary, use a salt water solution.

- Avoid using mouthwash to treat persistent bad breath. Halitosis (bad breath) may be the result of a problem that mouthwash can't cure, such as low grade infections in the nose, sinuses, tonsils, gums, or lungs, as well as from gastric reflux from the stomach.

- Consider using a microphone. In relatively static environments such as exhibit areas, classrooms, or exercise rooms, a lightweight microphone and an amplifier-speaker system can be of great help.

- Consider voice therapy. A speech-language pathologist who is experienced in treating voice problems can provide education on healthy use of the voice and instruction in proper voice techniques.

# IX. MARKETING YOURSELF

## Opportunities For Singers

The Occupational Outlook Handbook, 2010-11 Edition has this to offer on the current job outlook for singers:

## Musicians, Singers, and Related Workers

- Nature of the Work
- Training, Other Qualifications, and Advancement
- Employment
- Job Outlook
- Projections
- Earnings
- Wages
- Related Occupations
- Sources of Additional Information

## Significant Points

- Part-time schedules—typically at night and on weekends—intermittent unemployment, and rejection when auditioning for work are common; many musicians and singers supplement their income with earnings from other sources.
- Aspiring musicians and singers begin studying an instrument or training their voice at an early age.
- Competition for jobs, especially full-time jobs, is keen; talented individuals who can play several instruments and perform a wide range of musical styles should enjoy the best job prospects.

## Nature of the Work

Musicians, singers, and related workers play musical instruments, sing, compose or arrange music, or conduct groups in instrumental or vocal performances. They perform solo or as part of a group, mostly in front of live audiences in nightclubs, concert halls, and theaters. They also perform in recording or production studios for radio, TV, film, or video games. Regardless of the setting, they spend considerable time

90

practicing alone and with their bands, orchestras, or other musical ensembles.

*Musicians* play one or more musical instruments. Many musicians learn to play several related instruments and can perform equally well in several musical styles. Instrumental musicians, for example, may play in a symphony orchestra, rock group, or jazz combo one night, appear in another ensemble the next, and work in a studio band the following day. Some play a variety of string, brass, woodwind, or percussion instruments or electronic synthesizers.

*Singers* use their knowledge of voice production, melody, and harmony to interpret music and text. They sing character parts or perform in their own individual styles. Singers often are classified according to their voice range—soprano, contralto, tenor, baritone, or bass—or by the type of music they sing, such as rock, pop, folk, opera, rap, or country.

*Music directors* and *conductors* conduct, direct, plan, and lead instrumental or vocal performances by musical groups such as orchestras, choirs, and glee clubs. These leaders audition and select musicians, choose the music most appropriate for their talents and abilities, and direct rehearsals and performances. *Choral directors* lead choirs and glee clubs, sometimes working with a band or an orchestra conductor. Directors audition and select singers and lead them at rehearsals and performances to achieve harmony, rhythm, tempo, shading, and other desired musical effects.

*Composers* create original music such as symphonies, operas, sonatas, radio and television jingles, film scores, and popular songs. They transcribe ideas into musical notation, using harmony, rhythm, melody, and tonal structure. Although most composers and songwriters practice their craft on instruments and transcribe the notes with pen and paper, some use computer software to compose and edit their music.

*Arrangers* transcribe and adapt musical compositions to a particular style for orchestras, bands, choral groups, or individuals. Components of music—including tempo, volume, and the mix of instruments needed—are arranged to express the composer's message. Although some arrangers write directly into a musical composition, others use computer software to make changes.

***Work environment.*** Musicians typically perform at night and on weekends. They spend much additional time practicing or in rehearsal. Full-time musicians with long-term employment contracts, such as those with symphony orchestras or television and film production companies, enjoy steady work and less travel. Nightclub, solo, or recital musicians frequently travel to perform in a variety of local settings and may tour nationally or internationally. Because many musicians find only part-time or intermittent work and experience unemployment between engagements, they often supplement their income with other types of jobs. The stress of constantly looking for work leads many musicians to accept permanent full-time jobs in other occupations while working part time as musicians.

Most instrumental musicians work closely with a variety of other people, including colleagues, agents, employers, sponsors, and audiences. Although they usually work indoors, some perform outdoors for parades, concerts, and festivals. In some nightclubs and restaurants, smoke and odors may be present and lighting and ventilation may be poor.

## Training, Other Qualifications, and Advancement

Long-term on-the-job training is the most common way people learn to become musicians or singers. Aspiring musicians begin studying an instrument at an early age. They may gain valuable experience playing in a school or community band or orchestra or with a group of friends. Singers usually start training when their voices mature. Participation in school musicals or choirs often provides good early training and experience. Composers and music directors usually require a bachelor's degree in a related field.

***Education and training.*** Musicians need extensive and prolonged training and practice to acquire the skills and knowledge necessary to interpret music at a professional level. Like other artists, musicians and singers continually strive to improve their abilities. Formal training may be obtained through private study with an accomplished musician, in a college or university music program, or in a music conservatory. An audition generally is necessary to qualify for university or conservatory study. The National Association of Schools of Music is made up of 615 accredited college-level programs in music. Courses typically include music theory, music interpretation, composition, conducting, and performance, either with a particular instrument or a

92

voice performance. Music directors, composers, conductors, and arrangers need considerable related work experience or advanced training in these subjects.

A master's or doctoral degree usually is required to teach advanced music courses in colleges and universities; a bachelor's degree may be sufficient to teach basic courses. A degree in music education qualifies graduates for a State certificate to teach music in public elementary or secondary schools. (Information related to teachers—postsecondary and teachers—kindergarten, elementary, middle, and secondary can be found elsewhere in the Handbook.) Musicians who do not meet public school music education requirements may teach in private schools and recreation associations or instruct individual students in private sessions.

*Other qualifications.* Musicians must be knowledgeable about a broad range of musical styles. Having a broader range of interest, knowledge, and training can help expand employment opportunities and musical abilities. Voice training and private instrumental lessons, especially when taken at a young age, also help develop technique and enhance one's performance.

Young persons considering careers in music should have musical talent, versatility, creativity, poise, and good stage presence. Self-discipline is vital because producing a quality performance on a consistent basis requires constant study and practice. Musicians who play in concerts or in nightclubs and those who tour must have physical stamina to endure frequent travel and an irregular performance schedule. Musicians and singers also must be prepared to face the anxiety of intermittent employment and of rejection when auditioning for work.

*Advancement.* Advancement for musicians usually means becoming better known, finding work more easily, and performing for higher earnings. Successful musicians often rely on agents or managers to find them performing engagements, negotiate contracts, and develop their careers.

## Employment

Musicians, singers, and related workers held about 240,000 jobs in 2008, of which 186,400 were held by musicians and singers; 53,600 were music directors and composers. Around 43 percent worked part time; 50 percent were self-employed. Many found jobs in cities in which entertainment and recording activities are concentrated, such as New York, Los Angeles, Las Vegas, Chicago, and Nashville.

Musicians, singers, and related workers are employed in a variety of settings. Of those who earn a wage or salary, 33 percent were employed by religious, grantmaking, civic, professional, and similar organizations and 12 percent by performing arts companies, such as professional orchestras, small chamber music groups, opera companies, musical theater companies, and ballet troupes. Musicians and singers also perform in nightclubs and restaurants and for weddings and other events. Well-known musicians and groups may perform in concerts, appear on radio and television broadcasts, and make recordings and music videos. The U.S. Armed Forces also offer careers in their bands and smaller musical groups. (Information related to job opportunities in the armed forces can be found elsewhere in the Handbook.)

## Job Outlook

Employment is expected to grow as fast as average. Keen competition for jobs, especially full-time jobs, is expected to continue. Talented individuals who are skilled in multiple instruments and musical styles will have the best job prospects.

***Employment change.*** Employment of musicians, singers, and related workers is expected to grow 8 percent during the 2008–18 decade, as fast as the average for all occupations. Most new wage-and-salary jobs for musicians will arise in religious organizations. Slower than average employment growth is expected for self-employed musicians, who generally perform in nightclubs, concert tours, and other venues. The Internet and other new forms of media may provide independent musicians and singers alternative methods for distributing music.

***Job prospects.*** Growth in demand for musicians will generate a number of job opportunities, and many openings also will arise from the need to replace those who leave the field each year because they are unable to make a living solely as musicians or singers, as well as those who leave for other reasons.

Competition for jobs as musicians, singers, and related workers— especially full-time jobs—is expected to be keen. The vast number of people with the desire to perform will continue to greatly exceed the

94

number of openings. New musicians or singers will have their best chance of landing a job with smaller, community-based performing arts groups or as freelance artists. Instrumentalists should have better opportunities than singers because of a larger pool of work. Talented individuals who are skilled in multiple instruments or musical styles will have the best job prospects. However, talent alone is no guarantee of success: many people start out to become musicians or singers but leave the profession because they find the work difficult, the discipline demanding, and the long periods of intermittent unemployment a hardship.

*(End Abstract)*

## Recording and Commercials

There still exists many opportunities in local recording studios for singers to provide singing voice overs for commercials, but with the move toward home recording many vocalist-producers have gone to providing their own voice-overs as part of their studio package and so have tended less to use outside singers.

## The Music Biz Today

The tremendous changes which have occurred in the music industry in recent years have all but decimated a once thriving industry. The single largest blow to the business end of the recording industry has been the internet.

With the free downloading of recorded music on file sharing systems, the ability of artists to charge for the use of their recordings has been all but diminished.

Catastrophic economic downturns have crippled the live music business as well; even major artists have reported major drops in ticket sales as the world suffers from the latest economic crisis.

Yet there will still always remain the need for entertainers, singers to perform live music and singers to record. The economic realities for singers is uncertain, but one thing always remains: in any artistic endeavor, a creative artist continues to create and derives joy from the act itself, regardless of economic reward.

But for the singer who decides on a career in music to pay the bills, there are many hurdles.

## Age Considerations

In the entertainment world, economic success seems to go largely to the youth demographic. But some of the most successful touring acts of the present decade are, ironically, older artists.

We see classic rock acts like The Rolling Stones and Bruce Springsteen touring the world and see the demand has never been greater, and some speculate that when such rockers finally retire, there will be no acts to fill their shoes.

The point being is that you are never too old to rock and roll, and this is just another cool way of saying that age is in the mind - it's never too late to learn new things, create new experiences and live life to its fullest, and the pursuit of a singing career should be no exception.

## Travel Is Tough

One element of being a successful singer is that often performers must do extensive travelling and touring to make a living, and this kind of lifestyle can be extremely tiring.

Touring can create not only physical but mental exhaustion. Performers often relate that their family life suffers when they tour, and being away from home for extended periods of time can wreak havoc on marriages and relationships. Drug addiction, alcoholism and depression can accompany such a lifestyle, but this does not have to be.

Some singers make travelling a family affair, bringing their families on the road with them. Others schedule their touring dates so that they can return home every few weeks or so to spend time with their loved ones.

There are also many ways to make a living singing without touring, and in the end, the joy you get from performing locally - even singing in the shower - may be joy enough for you to pursue it.

## Styles - Change or Stay The Same?

Styles and fads come and go. Many singers who have had long careers have tried and changed different styles along the way. Elvis Presley, Johnny Mathis, even Frank Sinatra were among the many singers that recorded disks of many different styles of music.

Only you can decide what is right for you - but keep an open mind. A singer that can change styles is considered versatile - and any way you can add versatility and variety to your palette of colors as an artist can only be a good thing.

## Singing For Life

Singing is a lifelong pursuit. As of this writing some of the masters are still alive, singing and happy well into their 80's. Never give up thinking you are too old. Our great masters show us through their shining examples that age is only a state of mind.

## Beware the Charlatans!

It's the Wild wild west out there in the world of vocal instruction, particularly online, where a plethora of pages await to ensnare you in their web of deceit and greed.

View any information resource with scrutiny, especially one that wishes to take your money. There are all manner of "web courses," "internet lessons," "vocal methods" and more that are run by villains and charlatans ill-equipped to give you or anyone else instruction in anything other than taking people's money.

In the same manner, when shopping for a local instructor for live vocal instruction, it's just as important to pick someone with a verifiable pedigree as it is to find someone with whom you can relate to as a teacher.

## All teachers are not ideal for all students.

Find one that specializes in your particular style of interest, one who has helped others achieve at least some small level of success that you can reference.

Speak to other students who have graduated from this instructor's course of study, and be ever vigilant in choosing a teacher who you feel genuinely cares about your progress as a student, not just who wishes to take you through the paces and relieve you of your money.

I believe if you are a good judge of character you can spot a teacher who seems preoccupied with some distant dream while they are teaching - one who seems not in the moment - one who has a cool sense of detachment.

If you find yourself in the company of such a teacher, I would urge you to take your leave of their services and continue your search for the discovery of the one who speaks to your soul - one with whom you can relate to on some primary level.

You will know it when you have found the right teacher.

And if you have not found the right teacher, do not be afraid to go it alone. There are plenty of decent materials for you to get started learning your craft from qualified and well-reviewed courses of study that will serve you well, some contained in the Recommended Reading section of this book.

# CONCLUSION

No single book can hope to cover all the bases of singing and still hold the attention of the aspiring vocalist. This book has been my way of taking the very best of what I have learned about singing and put it into an easy to read, short, concise yet accurate and helpful guide that will place you on the road to a successful career in singing.

There are many other books on the subject, and if there are areas of interest I have not covered here, I offer the following resources as further research and reading.

Keep on singing, and I wish you much success, luck, happiness and pleasure as you venture down this amazing road of life.

# Recommended Reading

*Getting Gigs: The Musician's Survival Guide to Booking Better Paying Jobs (With or Without An Agent)* - Mark W. Curran
*Sell Your Music - How to Profitably Sell Your Own Recordings Online* - Mark W. Curran
*Singing for Dummies* - Pamelia S. Phillips
*Singing for the Stars: A Complete Program for Training Your Voice (Book & 2 CD's)* - Seth Riggs
*The Rock-N-Roll Singer's Survival Manual* - Mark Baxter
*Born to Sing: The Vocal Power Method Male and Female Voice All Styles* - Elisabeth Howard and Howard Austin
*The Everything Singing Book with CD:* - Bettina Sheppard
*Vocal Workouts for the Contemporary Singer* - Anne Peckham
*Singer's Handbook: A Total Vocal Workout in One Hour or Less!* - Anne Peckham

www.ingramcontent.com/pod-product-compliance
Lightning Source LLC
Chambersburg PA
CBHW071102090426
42737CB00013B/2439